Cold Heart

The Great Unsolved Mystery of
Turn of the Century Buffalo

Kimberly Tilley

Black Rose Writing | Texas

ISBN: 978-1-68433-604-3
PUBLISHED BY BLACK ROSE WRITING
www.blackrosewriting.com

Printed in the United States of America
Suggested Retail Price (SRP) $18.95

Cold Heart is printed in Garamond

*As a planet-friendly publisher, Black Rose Writing does its best to eliminate unnecessary waste to reduce paper usage and energy costs, while never compromising the reading experience. As a result, the final word count vs. page count may not meet common expectations.

Acknowledgements

The author gratefully thanks:

Dr. Richard Levy, whose guidance inspired me to write this book,
Charles Tilley and **Cynthia Van Ness,** Director of Library & Archives at the Buffalo History Museum, for generously sharing their specialized expertise,

Furman Walker, Kristin Sherry, Margaret Tilley, Harpreet Singh, Charlene Nuval, and **Alexis Keenan** for their excellent, thoughtful feedback that so vastly improved this book,

Ruwaida and Jamal Haddad, Isatu Bah, Amy McManus, Mayling and Dr. Lee, Emanuela Neagu, Todd Benson, Lily Suk, KT Thomas, Ashlee Wilkins, Blanca Batlle, Curt Peterson, Madeline Khurma, Loreen Brown, Jennifer-Bullock Shone, Patricia Rice, L.A. Townsend, Crystal Davies, Annick Strang, Nadia Buchko, and **Alexandra Balestrieri** for their friendship, enthusiasm, and advice,

Marcie Dean, for her encouragement and wisdom,

Mary Ginter, Beverly Pittenger, and **Sylvia and GA Wagner,** for supporting my writing,

Beth Crosby, whose editing talent is unsurpassed,

Reagan Rothe, founder of Black Rose Writing, for his partnership and innovative ideas,

Kristin Sherry, for her unshakeable confidence in me,

And always, great love and gratitude to **Mom** and **Pop.**

Author Note

This is the true story of one of the great unsolved murder mysteries of the early days of the twentieth century. The facts are presented as they unfolded during the investigation.

In 1903, the competition for readers amongst the large metropolitan daily papers was fierce. Newspaper editors featured sensationalized, exaggerated, and scandalous content with lurid headlines designed to seize potential readers' attention. Errors were common, and often rival newspapers covered the same event with significant factual differences.

This book is nonfiction and relies heavily on contemporaneous newspaper accounts. To ensure accuracy, the key facts related here were corroborated by multiple sources.

Cold Heart

Things are not always what they seem; the first appearance deceives many; the intelligence of a few perceives what has been carefully hidden.
— Phaedrus

Table of Contents:

Part 1

A Glittering Life in The City of Light

At the turn of the century, Buffalo, New York was ascendant. Its rapid growth was due, in part, to the city's importance as a strategic shipping location at the intersection of Lake Erie and the Niagara River. Immigrant laborers flocked to the city for jobs in the grain mills, lumber yards, and wire works. By 1900, the city's population swelled to more than 350,000 residents, making it the eighth largest city in the United States.

Buffalo hosted the Pan-American Exposition of 1901, and for the first time, the city stood in the international spotlight. The exposition was a display of human ingenuity in a classically beautiful setting. Hydroelectric power generated by nearby Niagara Falls illuminated the grounds with electricity, and dazzled visitors nicknamed Buffalo the "City of Light."

The exposition was also the tragic scene of President William McKinley's assassination. The popular president was shot twice by anarchist Leon Czolgosz during a public event at the Temple of Music. President McKinley was seriously wounded. He was taken to the Milburn House, where he and the first lady were staying during their visit.

When the president was known to be dying, Vice President Theodore Roosevelt rushed to the Milburn House. He arrived too late to see McKinley. Instead, he was sworn into office as the nation's president in the city of Buffalo, having served in the McKinley administration less than 200 days.

The country knew comparatively little about their new president, but they were hopeful. Roosevelt was truly a man of the age: optimistic, tough, and adventurous. It seemed apropos for this president to be sworn into office in a city that stood on the precipice of greatness.

In addition to attracting consequential visitors, Buffalo was home to many notable residents. Edwin Burdick was one of the city's most distinguished citizens. In 1903, the 40-year-old father of three was a success in every sense of the word.

Generous and friendly, Ed was a self-made man. He had started his career as a stenographer at an envelope manufacturing plant and worked his way up. When the owner of the plant retired, he sold the business to Ed and another employee, Charles Parke. Under their leadership, Buffalo Envelope Co. became one of the largest manufacturers of envelopes in the country. They produced more than 400,000 envelopes a day and employed seventy workers. Ed was also the president of his own publishing company, E. L. Burdick & Co.

Ed's physical stature was small, and his temperament humble. He enjoyed spending time with friends and family and had a lively interest in the lives of his friends. He was often described as an unusually compassionate man.

Ed married Alice Hull in 1885. Allie, as she was known to close friends and family, was a petite woman known for her impeccable taste in clothing. The Burdicks had three daughters: Marion, age 15; Carol, age 13; and Alice, age 10. Mrs. Burdick's parents lived with the family until the death of her father in 1899. James Hull left no money behind to support his widow, but thanks to her son-in-law's success, Mrs. Hull was financially secure. She remained with the family and helped to care for the girls.

The Burdicks lived in a large, beautiful home on fashionable Ashland Avenue in the Elmwood Village neighborhood, near Millionaire's Row. The family employed a full time cook and a maid, who lived on the third floor of the home.

101 Ashland Avenue

The names Alice and Edwin Burdick were fixtures in the society columns that chronicled the activities of the local gentry. Their names appear in numerous stories about upper crust dances, weddings, teas, and receptions, often accompanied by a description of the gown Alice wore to the event.

Ed and Alice were part of an insulated social group of about 20 wealthy couples, whom the press called the "Elmwood Avenue set." The group frequented the Red Jacket Golf Club, of which Ed was honorary president, and the Elmwood Avenue Dance Club.

There was a faint element of seediness about the Elmwood Avenue set. They were rumored to drink, throw wild parties, and generally behave in a way that was not altogether refined. However, these were only rumors. The group purposely kept their distance from their fellow citizens, which added to their mystique. Like a distant mountain range, their mansions and fantastic wealth created the backdrop of turn-of-the-century Buffalo.

In August 1902, Ed and Alice's eldest daughter, Marion, was profiled in the newspapers for an act of heroism. *The Morning News* explained that the girl had been driving alone in her father's electric wagon. "The interior insulation of the vehicle caught fire on Delaware Avenue near Johnson Park, and the brake refused to work. At a speed that sometimes exceeded 10 miles per hour … through some of the most crowded thoroughfares of Buffalo, crossing four double-track trolley lines … the distance being more than two miles … That no disaster resulted was due to the constant coolness displayed by the child." [1]

An electric carriage, circa 1901
Image Courtesy of EarlyAmericanAutomobiles.com

Steering a burning, out-of-control car through two miles of crowded city streets wouldn't be easy for anyone, let alone a young girl.

It makes for an interesting story, but the typical reader might have been more struck by the Burdick family's great wealth than the coolness displayed by their teenaged daughter. In 1903, the average annual income for a full-time worker was approximately $470, [II] while the average cost of an automobile was $625. [III] Few cars existed because only the very rich had the disposable income to buy and operate them.

Everything about the Burdicks—their marriage, family, home, and possessions—seemed perfect. Theirs was a life that others could only imagine.

Alice's Indiscretions

The elegant, polished image the Burdicks presented to the world was merely a façade, a smokescreen to disguise their volatile and unhappy marriage.

By February 1903, their divorce was imminent. It was the end of a long road that had begun two years earlier.

Alice and Edwin Burdick

In 1900, Ed and Alice were on especially good terms with three other couples in the Elmwood Avenue set. They often socialized with Seth and Gertrude Paine, J.B. and Helen Warren, and Arthur and Carrie Pennell.

The Pennells' lives would soon collide with the Burdicks in a fantastic way.

Arthur Reed Pennell was a likeable person with a romantic history. He was born aboard his father's ship on the South Pacific Ocean. John Pennell was a renowned sea captain, and Arthur, his parents, and his younger brother John traveled continually during the early years of his life. Captain Pennell died suddenly when Arthur was 13, and Mrs. Pennell took her sons to her family's home in Maine.

Arthur was highly intelligent and had a great appreciation for the arts and music. After college he attended Yale Law School, where he graduated with honors. He married Carrie Lamb in 1891, and the following year the couple moved to Buffalo.

The Pennells thrived in their adopted city. They quickly became friendly with the Burdicks and joined the Elmwood Avenue set. The Pennells had no children, but they liked the Burdicks' daughters. The Burdicks' children, in fact, placed no constraints on the time or behavior of their parents. Mrs. Hull did much of the parenting that would otherwise have been a demand upon Alice's time. Servants saw to their meals and picked up after them.

Ed got to know Arthur when they golfed together, and they became close friends. Like Ed, Arthur was intelligent, wealthy, and well-known. But some sharp differences separated the two. Whereas Ed was industrious and cheerful, Arthur was dreamy and brooding. Arthur was one of the foremost attorneys in Buffalo, but he was devoted to leisure and the finer things in life. And he could afford it. Through his wife, his law practice, and his extended family, he was surrounded by wealth.

In addition to spending time golfing and dancing, the Burdicks and the Pennells took short vacations together. The couples owned tandem bicycles and enjoyed riding together.

Far from feeling envious of his new friend, Ed admired Arthur. He trusted Pennell so completely, he had named him as the guardian of the children in his will, and the girls even called him Uncle Arthur. [iv]

Like Alice, Carrie Pennell was a noted socialite. Alice enjoyed socializing but Carrie threw herself into the role, joining organizations, hosting receptions, and planning afternoon teas nearly every week. By 1900, Mrs. Pennell was the leading socialite in Buffalo.

On New Year's Day 1901, the Pennells attended a festive gathering at the home of Edwin and Alice Burdick. Several other couples were there, but at one point during the evening, Carrie Pennell drew Ed aside. In a low voice, she informed him that Alice and Arthur were having an affair. She added that it had been going on for quite some time and that the two corresponded by letter frequently.

It's not clear how long Carrie knew about the affair before alerting Ed to it. Her purpose in telling him this devastating news was probably to enlist his help to break up the affair. Ed's reaction disappointed her. Initially, he could scarcely believe she was serious, then he was convinced she had simply made a grotesque mistake.

"They were together yesterday afternoon," Carrie told him impatiently.

Carrie Lamb Pennell, wife of Arthur Reed Pennell

Ed's thoughts turned to Alice. They had been married for sixteen years; they had three children together. It could not be. He stole a glance at Pennell. Arthur was tall and handsome, with an athletic build, just the opposite of Ed's shorter stature and small frame. It was conceivable that Alice would be attracted to him, but he never dreamed she would be unfaithful.

But Carrie's words ate away at him all evening. He found it difficult to join in the conversation and revelry.

As soon as the last guest left, Ed confronted his wife with what Carrie Pennell had told him. He was prepared for her to become angry or to laugh off the story, but Alice's reaction shocked him. She was defensive and evasive. Even the way she said Arthur Pennell's name seemed laden with meaning. He stared at her dully; it was true.

Carrie said that Alice and Arthur corresponded, and Ed demanded to see the letters. At first, Alice told him Arthur had never sent her any letters, and then she said he had, but she didn't keep them. Ed, following some obscure instinct, insisted he knew the letters existed, and finally Alice admitted she had them. She refused to show them to her husband, though.

In fact, she and Arthur corresponded by mail often. She had thrown away some of the letters, but most she treasured. For over two years, Alice checked the mail or intercepted the mailman every day to retrieve any letters from Arthur, and she kept his correspondence hidden away in a locked tin box.

Ed had seen the box, but he had never been curious about it. As he and Alice argued, he had a sudden flash of intuition. He was sure she was hiding the letters there. He retrieved the box from the closet and demanded Alice open it. She resisted, but Ed was insistent. Alice unwillingly unlocked the box.

Ed quickly skimmed a few of the letters in the box. There was no need for further confirmation for the tenor of the letters was unmistakable. Pennell referred to Alice as "my love, my life, my dearest one," and in another letter he told her he had found her misplaced gloves and continued, "Dearest, my darling, I kissed them because your hands were in them. I smoothed them out and kissed every finger because they had touched you."

Ed gave the box to Mrs. Hull for safekeeping and told Alice he was going away for a few days to think things over. He was a cautious man, mild-mannered and slow to act. He wanted a few days to himself to process what he had learned before deciding what steps he would take.

While Alice stayed home with her mother and the girls, Ed checked into a nearby hotel. He was deeply wounded. He had felt Alice's indifference toward him for some time but he had supposed her mind was occupied with social doings or the children. The truth made him miserable.

Alice was in shock. Her affair with Arthur started in 1898, when the Pennells invited the Burdicks to accompany them to New Haven, Connecticut, the city where they had met and married. Ed declined, explaining it was a busy time at work. His wife accepted and it was while visiting the Yale campus that she and

Arthur began a torrid affair. For two-and-a-half years, she and Arthur had continued their relationship and Ed had never suspected anything.

Nevertheless, the relationship had been exposed. Alice had no choice but to acknowledge the truth to her mother as well, since Ed had given Mrs. Hull the box of letters. She was preoccupied with the fact that Ed had forced her to open the tin box and give him the letters. "He took me by the throat and forced me to open it," she told her mother angrily. She turned to Arthur for comfort, but he told her she had been reckless to keep the letters.

A few days later, Ed returned. He thought he could forgive Alice for the affair, if they could really put it behind them. However, he had no intention of being duped again, and he soon suspected that his wife had not ended the affair with Arthur Pennell.

One afternoon, he deliberately came home early and found Alice was out. When his wife returned, he immediately began to question her. Alice, flustered, admitted she had been out walking with Pennell.

This time, Ed packed his things and announced he was moving out for good. He was deaf to his wife's protests and pleading to remain in their home. The Genesee Hotel was rapidly upgrading to attract visitors to the Pan-American Exposition. Ed moved into a luxury suite.

Her husband was staying less than two miles from their home, but Alice was desperate for him to move back home. She sent one letter after another, pleading for Ed's forgiveness, cajoling him to come home, and promising to avoid Pennell.

The Genesee, where Edwin Burdick lived briefly in 1901

Ed stayed away for a week or two, but he soon acceded to his wife's wishes and came home, determined to reconcile with her.

If Alice's affair with Arthur Pennell ceased when Ed moved to the Genesee—and no evidence suggests it did—their relationship resumed immediately. Despite the appeals she made to her husband to avoid breaking up their family, Alice Burdick was uninterested in ending her affair with Arthur Pennell. They did, however, attempt a degree of discretion. They were more careful about when and where they met, and no more love letters from Pennell arrived at the Burdick home. Arthur Pennell was uneasy when he learned Ed had taken his letters and worried continually that they would one day resurface in some humiliating way. Alice assured him there would be no further trouble; she was confident that her husband had been pacified.

But they underestimated Ed, who proved to be far more resourceful than either of them guessed. He was hypervigilant but took care to conceal his suspicion. By March 1901, Ed was convinced that Pennell was still corresponding with his wife.

Acting on a hunch, he went to the post office and introduced himself as Alice Burdick's brother. He told the clerk his sister had a post office box there, and she wanted him to have access to it.

Ed's instinct was correct. The clerk confirmed Alice Burdick had procured a post office box a few months earlier, and he willingly handed over a duplicate key.

Ed opened the box, already knowing what he would find. He pulled out a stack of envelopes, addressed to his wife from her lover, written after he had discovered the amorous letters in the tin box. Ed read through each letter rapidly. Each communication contained Pennell's memories of liaisons with Alice, and his declarations of love were unmistakable.

> *Am I foolish to want to telephone you from way down here just for the happiness of hearing your dear voice and especially when I am no good at all at talking over the telephone? It is worth all it costs to me and if gives you happiness in the least, then I am doubly repaid, for I love you, dear, more than you can know. More and more do I realize and know that you are the only woman in the world for me.*

Ed grimaced as he read a letter that referenced "the paradise in your arms." The discovery made him feel wretched, and he struggled to accept the enormity of his wife's treachery. Not only had Alice continued her affair with Arthur; he now understood that she never had any intention of ending it.

Ed's cautious nature conquered any emotional wish he may have felt to confront Alice and Arthur. He kept the discovery to himself and continued to turn up at the post office regularly to check the box and read Pennell's letters.

Ed often read the mail before Alice did. Not wanting his wife to know he was aware of her deception, he steamed the letters open, copied their text, then replaced the sealed envelopes in the box. The information he gathered from the letters, supplemented by his keen observations, painted an ugly picture of his wife.

At times, he learned of their meetings, though he wasn't sure of exact locations. Despite sending his letters to a location he didn't think Ed would ever find, Pennell still exercised caution by using coded references, such as: "I will meet you at 1, 2, 3 Wednesday morning."

Alice Burdick was a bold woman. She was confident that her reassurances had overcome any lingering suspicions her husband may have harbored since he returned home from the Genesee. She was so sure of herself that one spring afternoon, without any fanfare, she removed her wedding band and replaced it with a ring Arthur Pennell had given her.

Ed shattered her complacency in mid-May 1901 when he suddenly confronted her with the knowledge that she and Arthur were still seeing each other. Alice denied it, but her husband immediately countered with enough information to remove any possibility he was bluffing.

Alice was completely unprepared for Ed's demand that she leave the family home. Reeling, and with no grounds upon which to defend herself, she reluctantly agreed.

A Good Girl

Now exiled, Alice Burdick grew frantic. At least when Ed had moved into the hotel, she had been able to stay at home with her family, and she had plenty of money and servants to wait on her. Now she was living alone, more than 400 miles away, in an Atlantic City hotel room.

She wrote to her husband several times every week, sometimes twice a day. Her letters followed two themes: the toll Ed's unprovoked cruelty was taking on her and the harm he was doing to their innocent children.

To an uninitiated observer, Alice's letters give the impression that she was the injured victim. Her words were taunting and coaxing, by turns, but her aim never changed. Alice wanted to come home. Her letter dated May 22 made that clear.

> *You did not realize the effect your telegram would have upon me or you would not have done what you did. However, I do not reproach you. I am cut adrift with very small resources. I certainly hoped to make one more appeal to you in person before you left, which you probably anticipated and avoided.*
>
> *If I come back, I will not see or communicate in any way with Arthur; I'll be a loyal wife and mother. He said he will comply with anything I wish regarding our future and carry out any promise I make. If you say I am not to come back, my only course is to appeal to him for protection. What my future will be, if Carrie refuses to free him, will be too dreadful.*
>
> *I will not appeal to you through the children. They will do that for themselves later, when it is too late, probably. As you say you will only think of yourself from now on, it rests with you to decide.*
>
> *I have more respect and honor for you than I ever had. Who can say what the future might bring? Severing the tie is much harder*

*than I thought. The companionship of fifteen years brought us so
much. It wrings my heart when I think of those blessed babies!*

*But I don't intend to work on your feelings. If you have any
heart, answer at once. I am not at all well this morning; so weak that
I could hardly get up.*

In one letter, Ed intimated that he would allow Alice to return, under the
condition that Pennell leave Buffalo. He pointed out that if Arthur really would
do anything for her, then he would leave the city if she asked. If he left by mid-
June, Alice could come back for the sake of the children and her mother.

"If he refuses your request, you will accept the situation without complaint
or regret," he wrote. "You should be willing to abide by any action taken by the
man whose love you exchanged for your husband's honor." He added that he
was prepared to fight for full custody of the children.

But Alice's reply made it clear the Pennells had no plans to leave Buffalo.

*Arthur says they invited several guests during the summer and it
will be absolutely impossible for them to leave; but he will
probably leave in the fall. You realize the matter rests between
yourself and Arthur. I am powerless to change it. I only promise
to keep faith with you and he will help me do it. We know that
if I come back we must give each other up.*

The last part of her letter shifted in tone completely.

*Don't you think it would be better for you to come here, where
we could talk rather than write? Perhaps I could make you see
things differently if you were here. There are some things might
be talked over and better decided upon if you were to come here.*

Ed wavered. In his response, he asked his wife to try to see things from his
point of view.

*Can't you understand that while Arthur remains in Buffalo,
I've no confidence in you? You've done everything to prove you*

cannot be trusted. You love him and you have no love for me. Have I ever reproached you?

If I were a woman and loved a man as you say you loved him, I would doubtless do as you have done, but I would be prepared to accept the consequences without complaint.

Alice continued to flood her husband with letters, which seemed to taunt Ed with Arthur's eagerness to see her while promising to become a devoted wife and never to see him again.

Even as she begged for another chance, an undercurrent of anger was detectable in her writing.

Arthur's telegram this morning says he will be away most of the summer and will probably leave in the fall. He asks if I want him to come here. I told him I would write to you again and he is waiting to hear your decision.

I will return if I may and be as good a wife and mother as it is possible to be. I will do all, perhaps more, than I promise. I'll never voluntarily see or communicate with Arthur. I'm sure he will be too glad to leave the city in the fall.

You know your own mind as well today as you will later. Tell me at once. If I am coming home, I want to come now. I've had enough of this place. Marion wrote and said mama isn't well and Carol is so unhappy I am away that she couldn't eat breakfast. Little Alice has just begun her life, she needs her mother to guide her. You must not be so unkind to the children and keep me away. They'll suffer for so many years. I've made every effort, now I'm sick in mind and in body and this is almost more than I can endure here, all alone.

Such a grave question should not be decided by letter. But you evidently thought differently or you wouldn't have left me as you did. If I told you my feelings toward you have changed during this separation, you would scoff so let me come back and see what a good girl I will be. Please write me at once, I am so lonesome.

The response from Ed is a portrait of a complex man who was angry and hurt—and torn. He did not believe a reconciliation was possible. He sensed he was being manipulated. He did not think Pennell would leave Alice alone, nor did he believe his wife wished to be free of her lover. But he was weakening under the sustained assault on his feelings. His May 27 letter reflected his irresolute state of mind.

> *What is there to look forward to in life for a man whose wife loves another man, with the constant presence of that lover? I love my children, I am willing to sacrifice for them, but I'm not heroic and a future of this kind is not attractive.*
>
> *Suppose I should find it impossible to love and respect you, and treat you as a wife should be treated, wouldn't you be happier with the man you do love and who loves you?*
>
> *How could you make me happy when you love another man and must think of him constantly? You never tried during the years before you knew him and I loved you long after your indifference ought to have killed that love. If you really tried, you could even now win back my love and respect, but I cannot stand this strain.*

As to the children, Ed promised to be generous. His heart hurt for them, but he pointed out that Alice could have thought of them too, when she replaced her wedding ring with one given to her by Arthur. "I fear you simply wish to come here until he can free himself from his wife; then you will go to him," he concluded.

Ed was inclined to let Alice return. He wanted their daughters to have their mother, and he was keenly aware that the girls would be stigmatized if their parents divorced. It was also awkward having Mrs. Hull living in the house, when her daughter had been banished to Atlantic City. Ed reluctantly admitted to himself that a part of him missed his wife and wished she would come home.

Yet each time he was on the brink of allowing Alice to come back, something happened that caused him to stop short. Soon after posting his last letter to Alice, he received a brief note from Carrie Pennell, asking him to drop by. He went to see her willingly, but left after Carrie informed him that Arthur was contemplating filing a countersuit against him, alleging he had been unfaithful to Alice.

When he got home, Ed sent Alice an uncharacteristically blunt reply to her most recent letter, telling her of the conversation with Carrie.

> *I told Carrie I was considering whether to bring suit against you for divorce at once. She informed me of the threat to involve others. She said Arthur received a letter from you on Thursday and that he would go to you on Monday. She seemed to be familiar with everything and I have no doubt her interview with me was with his knowledge, or at his direction.*
>
> *His threat comes from you, of course. You leave me only one course to pursue. For the sake of my children it is a hard one, but I have to fight for what little honor your conduct has left me and I will fight the rest of my life for them.*
>
> *As you intend to bring countercharges against me, the case will have to be tried in open court. If the truth prevails, there can be only one result in the public mind, as well as the verdict of the jury.*

He signed the letter formally: Yours truly, Edwin L. Burdick.
Alice sent a frantic response.

> *I am simply stunned by your letter! Those things had never entered my mind. I know nothing about what Carrie said. There has been no word exchanged between Arthur and I regarding charges against you; there has never been a word between us regarding any relations between you and anyone of a serious nature. We have laughed about your friendship with certain people but only what you have heard many times from all of your friends.*
>
> *I wrote Arthur your final answer and he said he would, of course, come to me. He is coming to Atlantic City tonight and I shall see him tomorrow. I wanted to see you, but you would not come. It's only right that I should see Arthur and*

find out what all this means. Perhaps I can change his mind about leaving Buffalo.

I will not say that you are wrong, but I would have kept my promises to you and his pride would have prompted him to give me up entirely and absolutely. We were prepared to do that! When he said he would not promise to leave Buffalo, what was I to do?

Tell me, Ed, if I should come back to you and say I wanted to stay—oh so much—would you send me away again? Haven't you any wish for me at all? Have I gone entirely out of your heart? I cannot do much more with letter writing. My head is in such a state and you ought not to expect it.

"Do nothing until you hear from me. I say this in the interest of us both," Alice wrote in closing. She was too late. On June 6, she received a legal notice, informing her Ed was bringing a divorce suit against her. ^v

She wrote to him resentfully that evening.

I was more than surprised to receive a letter from your lawyers, stating the action you had taken—an action that I supposed we agreed was to be avoided. I have seen Arthur today but I am suffering from a splitting headache, I don't feel I can write tonight. I will write tomorrow when I hope to feel better.

Arthur Pennell sought out Ed. He was incensed about Ed's threat to divorce Alice and urgently advised him not to proceed. Burdick's demeanor under pressure was as slow and deliberate as Arthur's was warm and impetuous. He quietly said he had considered all options and was convinced that divorcing Alice was the best way to move forward. Arthur alternately argued and pleaded with him and finally threatened to kill himself if Ed did not relent. ^{vi}

Arthur Reed Pennell, Alice Burdick's lover

"Brace up," Ed told him brusquely. "You've always had a choice in the matter, Arthur. If you would leave town for good, I would drop the divorce suit."

This, Arthur refused to consider. He valued his reputation above nearly everything—everything except, perhaps, his love for Alice Burdick. Perhaps that was why he neither pursued a divorce from his own wife, nor ended his affair with Alice.

Yet, mysteriously, Ed dropped the divorce proceedings. He agreed to allow Alice to come home, despite the Pennells remaining in town. She returned to Buffalo, rapturously happy, in mid-June 1901.

Ed had warned his wife that he did not trust her, and his suspicions were soon justified. Alice's behavior had not changed. She was no more attentive to Ed and the children than she had ever been. Soon after her return, Ed checked the post office box and found new letters from Arthur, written since her return.

The affair had never ended, and no matter what promises she had made, Alice obviously had no intention of avoiding her paramour.

The tension between Alice and Ed increased as time went on. Weeks and months passed, punctuated by fierce quarrels. By the end of 1901, the threat of divorce was again a daily consideration.

1902

More than a year had passed since Ed had become aware of Alice's affair, and he was sure it had never ceased.

He and Alice continued to squabble. After a particularly angry exchange in late January, Ed left town for business travel. He sent his wife a letter from his Indianapolis hotel dated January 29. In it, he noted Arthur had written to him, requesting a meeting, but that he was resolved to move forward with a divorce. Much of his letter was bitter.

> *Pennell says your interest is greater than mine. His interests are certainly paramount to those of the family he has finally succeeded in completely breaking up. I am well aware this means my social ruin, so an interview to tell me this would be no good.*
>
> *Several weeks ago, I decided upon February 3 to begin the divorce suit. I put it off as long as I could, thinking he might conclude to leave the city. He has not, so the date will not be changed.*
>
> *I'll be in Buffalo on Saturday and wish to see the children on Sunday. It will be hard to tell them I am not coming home again. I leave it to you to tell them why.*

In her response, Alice adopted the role of an abandoned wife who was relentlessly pursued by another man, through no fault of her own.

> *Will nothing move you from the terrible determination you made? Your letter came this morning and, needless to say, I am crushed completely. I asked Mr. Pennell to leave Buffalo, although his going has been delayed.*

I thought you would return to us. How can you bring this terrible thing upon us? For our darling children, won't you be generous? For the love of our children, even if you have no love for me. They need your protection, and they need the care that I can give them. This will completely crush them.

I cannot, will not believe that you have it in your heart to bring this terrible thing upon them. My God, Ed, this cannot, must not be. You cannot be so cruel as to bring this upon us. You have been generous and must be so now. I am nearly crazy, but I must be brave for the children.

The day Ed returned to Buffalo, Alice appeared at his office, and she did not leave until she persuaded him to come home. The divorce suit was not mentioned, and February 3 passed without Ed taking any action.

As the months passed, Alice slid back into a comfortable routine similar to the one she had before Ed learned of the affair. Whenever Arthur Pennell's name came up, she assured her husband their affair was over. She lied with impunity, as it did not occur to her that Ed could've learned of the post office box or gotten access to it.

Alice was too preoccupied to give much thought to Ed. She had recently noticed that Arthur was seriously depressed. When he was away, he wrote frequently. Though still filled with protestations of love, his letters were laced with heavy sadness. During a trip to his boyhood home in Maine, he wrote, "I love you and I want you, but you are not with me, nor ever will be. I am unhappy, hopeless, heavy-hearted, and apathetic … Fate is inexorable unless we choose to break it."

Another letter, written a few weeks later, was even more despondent.

You do not know and never can, how much I love you … I do not think you feel as strongly and intensely as I do. If you did, nothing could keep us apart, and it is not right that we should be kept apart … I feel we shall drift until that fate which I feel so strongly in my heart is ours, separates us forever and saves you for your children, from me at least, and so I shall go on despairingly… such has always been the

feeling deep in my heart and that the time is not far distant…
I should be willing to die for an hour with you.

Arthur likely destroyed Alice's letters to him, so it's difficult to gauge how eager she was to be with him. His letters suggest he cared more for her than she did for him.

Meanwhile, unbeknownst to Alice, her husband was reading and copying each letter.

The Last Straw

By late 1902, Ed was no longer interested in reconciling with Alice. Their fighting had become frequent and acrimonious, and he was tired of it. His focus shifted to gathering the necessary evidence to support a divorce suit. In addition to continuing to copy Pennell's letters to Alice, he hired a private detective to trail the couple.

By the end of November, the detective reported that he had more than enough evidence for Ed to obtain a divorce on the grounds that his wife was an adulteress. Among other things, the detective learned Arthur and Alice met in places all over the city, including a furnished apartment Pennell had rented specifically to rendezvous with Alice. In the proof the detective provided, Ed soon saw that his darkest suspicions about his wife were only incorrect in that they did not go far enough.

A profile photograph of Ed, taken about 1902

The final straw came when the detective learned that Alice and Arthur had plans to meet at the Seventh Street apartment on Tuesday, December 2. It was the first time he had managed to learn of their plans in advance. Ed, no longer tormented by mixed feelings, was eager to force a confrontation. He arranged to meet the detective and his partner at the apartment, shortly after Alice and Pennell arrived.

On December 2, Ed stood outside the apartment door with the detectives for several minutes listening, and he was sure he detected voices inside. He pounded on the door. They heard scuffling, and at length Pennell opened the door and peered across the threshold. Ed demanded to see his wife.

His former friend feigned surprise. "Why should Alice be here?"

When Ed insisted on speaking with Alice a second time, Pennell said she was not there. He stepped back, pulling the door open wide to admit the men. "Come in and see for yourself," he offered. Ed pushed past him and looked around the apartment, but it was clear Alice was not there.

Ed went to his office, and returned home at his usual time. He found Alice at home, and the family preparing for dinner. He took his place across the table from her and watched her as she ate and calmly chatted with her mother and the girls.

After dinner, he followed her to the back parlor where the family generally sat after dinner. Alice perched on a striped chair and demurely picked up her book. They were alone for the moment and Ed came to her side.

When she looked up, he asked, "Where were you today, Allie?"

She looked at him with her black eyes that had so intrigued him when they met years ago. At the time, they were bright and expressive. Now they were merely blank as she answered, "At church."

"You were not at church," Ed stated flatly. "You were with Pennell at that apartment."

Alice looked him in the eye. There were no pretenses between them now. "I didn't know it was you at the door. If I had, I would've let you in myself."

"I told you I wouldn't overlook it again," Ed said slowly. "And I won't. This time you're leaving this house for good."

Alice's eyes widened, and she rose hastily. "Ed, you can't—"

Ed cut her off. "You can stay here tonight, but you must pack your things and go. Tomorrow you will be on the early train, and you will never return to this house."

Alice telephoned Arthur and told him that Ed was insisting she leave. "Never mind," he told her. "Just pack your things. We'll go to Niagara Falls tomorrow."

That evening, Alice packed her trunk and a satchel. Ed slept in a guest room.

The next day, December 3, Alice was on a north-bound train with a one-way ticket in her bag. She did not inform her daughters or mother that Ed had ordered her to leave; rather, she simply said she was going on a trip to Niagara Falls. Arthur Pennell accompanied her, and she checked in to the Prospect Park Hotel. According to Alice, he visited daily, but he did not stay with her there.

Alice made one trip back to Buffalo for a dental appointment, and she arranged to meet her mother while she was in town. When they met, Mrs. Hull revealed Ed had told her that "he had found his wife in a situation he could not overlook." [VII]

Mrs. Hull wanted to know what Alice's plans were. From Buffalo, she planned to go to New York City for two weeks, her daughter replied. At the end of that time, she hoped Ed would allow her to come home.

After her brief visit, Arthur joined her at the train station to escort her to New York City. Alice obtained a room at Hotel Roland, an establishment that fit her budget nicely but might not have met her ordinary standards. A contemporaneous ad for Hotel Roland clearly lists the pricing and specifies that the hotel desires refined, cultured, and nice guests.

Pennell traveled home to Buffalo the next morning. He would return in a few days with his wife to spend a short holiday in the city at the famed Waldorf Astoria hotel. The Waldorf did not have to warn away unsuitable potential guests in this way; their prices ensured only the wealthiest people could afford to stay there.

An advertisement for Hotel Roland

In the early days of December, friends of Ed Burdick noticed a change in him. He appeared to be jumpy. He confided to a few people, including his close friend and business partner Charles Parke, that he feared for his life. He did not elaborate, but Parke urged his friend to take precautions. A few days later, Burdick purchased a revolver that he carried everywhere.

Ed met briefly with Pennell while the latter was in Buffalo. Arthur announced he was Alice's legal representation for the divorce and attempted to intercede for her. Burdick, no doubt irritated by the situation, told him bluntly that he was not interested in a reconciliation. Arthur left without feeling much concern. Ed would come around, he felt sure of that.

But Ed, it seemed, was seeing his wife in a new light and felt she had played him for a fool. From the time he had learned of Alice's affair with Arthur, they had been like two actors playing the same scene over and over. He would demand she end the affair and attempt to punish her in some way. She would plead and promise to change. Eventually, Ed would forgive her and agree to give her another chance. Inevitably, evidence would surface that the relationship between Alice and Arthur was ongoing, and the scene would begin again.

Despite the deep wounds Alice inflicted upon him, Ed had always taken his wife back because he loved her and believed that preserving their marriage was best for the children. Yet even during their reconciliations, he was never at ease; he distrusted Alice and was acutely ashamed of her conduct.

The curtain had come down on their dismal drama for the last time on the day he went to Pennell's apartment on Seventh Street. As he stood outside the apartment door with the detectives, straining to hear voices inside, he realized that even the pain of a divorce was less torturous than the agony Alice's actions were causing him.

Two weeks after he ordered his wife to leave, Ed retained George C. Miller as legal counsel and petitioned for divorce on the grounds that Alice committed adultery. It's worth noting that the state of New York's anti-adultery laws considered the affair between Alice and Arthur to be a criminal offense. [VIII] Most divorce suits filed on grounds of adultery named a corespondent with whom the spouse was accused of having an affair. Ed named Arthur Pennell as the corespondent in the Burdick's divorce.

The Waldorf-Astoria (circa 1900) was called "the finest hotel in the world." [IX]

Detroit Publishing Co., Copyright Claimant, and Publisher Detroit Publishing Co. The Waldorf-Astoria, New York. Photograph. Retrieved from the Library of Congress, <www.loc.gov/item/2016801904/>

On Christmas Eve, Ed received a letter with the return address of the Waldorf Astoria. He opened it curiously.

The letter was from Carrie Pennell, dated December 22. She had written hastily, and her beautiful handwriting was unusually rough.

> *Eddie—are you absolutely crazy that you are willing to take the whole responsibility of this affair into your own hands? Arthur tells me that you refuse to make any difference, no matter what concessions he makes. If so, the burden rests with you and you are sacrificing more than you dream of.*
>
> *All you are asked to do is to have Allie home for Christmas. The children want her so much. If you don't, think what that might mean. Arthur doesn't regard life any too highly. He knows Allie could never be happy separated from the children, no matter how he might want to make her so. You know his romantic nature, how it would appeal to him to go and take her with him. Consider the awfulness of it before it is too late.*
>
> *I believe it, Eddie, or I would not write. I beg you once more to listen to reason.*

It seems bold for Carrie Pennell to insert herself into the Burdicks' domestic affairs and attempt to redirect their course of action. Taken at face value, her letter suggests that if Ed didn't take his wife back, Arthur would kill Alice and himself. Another interpretation might be that Carrie worried about the potential consequences of the Burdicks' divorce. She may have feared Arthur would divorce her to be with Alice.

Mrs. Pennell's thoughts and emotions are a mystery. She had known of the affair for years, but there's no evidence she attempted to put an end to it, beyond alerting Ed. While they were on vacation in New York City, Carrie was well aware that Arthur visited Alice Burdick every day at the Hotel Roland. Despite the misery of her situation, Mrs. Pennell appeared unwilling to leave her husband.

Ed sent an exasperated reply to her, explaining he had already taken his wife back three times, and would not do so again. His petition for divorce was scheduled to be on the court docket during the first week of March 1903, and he had no doubt of its success. As he wrote, he felt an unexpected sense of relief in knowing that within 10 weeks, their marriage would finally be dissolved. And, though he did not inform Carrie or anyone else of it, Ed had already written a new will that cut Alice off completely.

A few days after Christmas, another letter from Alice arrived, dated December 28, written from Hotel Roland. Ed noted, with some satisfaction, that his wife's accommodations were not quite so posh as the ones the Pennells were enjoying at the Waldorf Astoria.

Alice wrote that Arthur told her of his meeting with Ed and his intent to seek a divorce. "Is there no alternative?" she wrote. "I ask for the children's sake, for they are more to me than they are to you." Alice expressed her intent to go to Atlantic City by midweek and added, "I am not very well and I suppose everyone would be better off if I were well out of the way. Please do not send me such a bitter letter as the last."

Ed did not respond. His sister, Genevieve Stowell, passed away on December 29, after a long illness. Her death was hard for Ed, though his sister's death was expected. He spent the day helping his brother-in-law, Fitch Stowell, make funeral arrangements.

When he returned to his office the following day, he found Carrie Pennell had sent another letter to him there. Again, she pleaded Alice's case:

> *I've always said your conduct has been splendid. That's why I want to make a final appeal to you to close out the old year with an act of kindness.*
>
> *Allie wants to come back and she is a good mother to the children. No one knows! Your honor and hers will be saved and the children will be spared. If she wants to return and you refuse, the responsibility for the shame and the disgrace that fall upon the children is yours.*
>
> *I appeal to you to take their mother back.*

She ended by saying, *"The hardest thing of all is to live with regret."*

Ed looked up from the letter as his friend Charles Parke entered the office. For a few minutes, he vented about the situation. Carrie had told him of the affair in the first place, he told Parke. "If she'd only kept quiet, none of this would have happened."

It was a curious sentiment that suggested Ed would have preferred to remain ignorant of his wife's indiscretions, and that had he been able to do so, they wouldn't have had any trouble. Regardless of whether that was true, he was determined to act now.

Desperate Measures

On January 1, 1903, Alice Burdick arrived in Atlantic City and established a transient residence at the lavish Traymore Hotel. The irony of the date was not lost on her. It was two years to the day from the time Ed learned of her affair with Arthur Pennell.

Now she was far away from her daughters, her mother, her husband, and her home, and her future looked bleak. Matters with Arthur were uncertain. She had few possessions to her name beyond what was in the bureau in her Atlantic City hotel room. Letters from her mother kept her abreast of what was happening with the children at home, but there was no message from Ed.

In mid-January, Alice convinced Ed to meet her at the Genesee Hotel in Buffalo for a talk, but she didn't achieve the outcome she desired. Ed was not inclined to linger. He merely told her that she could have custody of the children for half the year if she married Pennell and didn't contest the divorce. He was unmoved by her tears.

Once back in Atlantic City, Alice continued to write to Ed, pleading to be taken back and allowed to come home.

Alice's protestations of sorrow and shame were obviously untrue. Atlantic City was an interesting place and, freed from the detective's spying eyes, she could see Arthur openly. He frequently visited her there and offered sanguine assurances that Ed would relent soon and let her return to Buffalo. But they both had plenty of reason to doubt that would be the case.

Certainly, Alice's reasons for wanting to return to Buffalo were suspect. It was likely she missed her posh lifestyle much more than her family. Ed had accused her more than once of staying with him only until she could be secure of Arthur. Alice denied this, but it was perfectly true.

Arthur promised that he would divorce Carrie, at which point he and Alice would go out west and start a new life together and put Ed behind them for good. Until that day came, Alice had always been able to smooth things over with promises of reformed conduct. She was confident in her power over her husband and believed things would play out again the way they always had. Alice seemed to despise Ed for his forgiving nature, though all of her plans relied on it.

But something was wrong. Every day, she looked in vain for a letter from him telling of his pain and admitting that he missed her too. Ed, busy in Buffalo, no longer felt susceptible to his wife's entreaties. He disregarded the growing pile of apologetic, tear-stained letters from Alice promising things would really be different this time, if he only took her back again.

Alice Hull Burdick

When her letters continued to go unanswered, Alice's anxiety became palpable, and it finally compelled Arthur to act. In late January, he appeared unannounced at Ed's office. He attempted to persuade him to drop the divorce suit, initially attempting to make light of the affair. Burdick had to take Alice back, he reasoned. She was his wife, after all. To Arthur's surprise and displeasure, he found his former friend to be as stony and unyielding as Alice had indicated.

Burdick bluntly refused Pennell's repeated requests and demands to allow Alice to come home. As they spoke, Arthur realized Ed knew much more about their relationship than he or Alice had thought possible. Ed informed him that he had hired a detective and calmly talked through some of the evidence the man had gathered, including the locations where Pennell and Alice had secretly met, a romantic weekend they had spent in Niagara Falls, and a lavish suite they had shared at the Waldorf-Astoria Hotel in New York City.

However, Ed was ready to offer a truce. If Alice and Arthur would marry and keep a decent home, he would forgive them. He would even willingly share custody of their daughters.

It was a generous offer—and a crafty one. Alice had told Ed that Pennell had promised to get a divorce and marry her. Alice might have believed it, but Ed suspected Arthur had no intention of divorcing his wife. Though he no longer wanted to reconcile with his wife, Ed's wounded vanity took some solace in the hope that Alice would soon realize what a tremendous mistake she had made.

Arthur's tone became desperate. "Don't you realize what a divorce will do?" he cried, his voice rising. "It will ruin all of us! You have to consider your children." Ed must be decent and drop the divorce suit, he insisted.

Ed folded his arms and gazed at Pennell. He would not be threatened, he said. If Arthur attempted to force his hand, he would not hesitate to publish the love letters he had discovered.

This was Arthur's Achilles' heel. The box of letters Burdick had seized on New Year's Day 1901 had always worried him. He had always feared they would resurface and be used to humiliate him. His anxiety would have heightened tenfold had he known Ed had copies of the letters from the post office box.

"I won't have her back." Ed's voice was low, but it shook with anger. "I warned both of you. I warned you over and over."

Pennell leaped to his feet. His face was scarlet, and a vein bulged on his forehead. "You must take her back! You *will* take her back. If you don't, I'll kill myself, but not before I kill both of you!"

Ed said nothing. He felt as though a frost covered his heart, and his emotions were on ice.

Arthur glowered at him, hating him for his icy composure and his cold, methodical manner. "I mean what I say." He put on his hat and left, shutting the door with a bang behind him.

This incident highlights the conflicting nature of what is known about Arthur Pennell. In some respects, he seems selfish, opportunistic, and calculating. That was certainly what Ed Burdick believed to be true. At other times, though, he seems to be genuine and deeply in love with Alice Burdick. In several of his letters, he mentions her love for her children and laments that she could never be completely happy with him if the children were estranged from her. Whether Arthur's assessment of Alice's feelings was accurate is unknown.

Arthur reported some of the details of the conversation to Alice but told her not to worry. He had formulated a plan. He regretted losing his temper in Ed's office, but as it turned out, he had not put all of his cards on the table. His former friend was not the only person capable of gathering information through surveillance. For more than a year, Arthur Pennell had hired two detectives to shadow Ed Burdick. [x] The information they provided laid the groundwork for the plan Arthur shared.

Alice would not contest the divorce; rather she would launch a countersuit, alleging Ed had been unfaithful to her with *three* other women.

The first was Mrs. Helen Warren. Before she married, Helen Cleveland lived in Buffalo, where she was friendly with the Burdicks. Four years ago, she married J. Burton Warren, and the couple lived in Buffalo before returning to his hometown of Cleveland, Ohio.

Mrs. Warren was said to be charming by all who knew her, but her marriage was an unhappy one. She recently returned to her father's home and was in the process of divorcing Warren. Ed had often spoken of his admiration of Mrs. Warren.

The second woman was described as a prominent local socialite. Though Alice would not use her name, it would be understood by the Elmwood Avenue set that she was referring to Gertrude Paine. Mrs. Paine was a beautiful woman and the wife of Seth Paine, the dentist. Dr. Paine worked in Batavia and stayed there during the week, leaving Mrs. Paine to attend to household matters and finances—an area in which she frequently required assistance. Alice knew that Mrs. Paine was friendly with her husband and that he had given her money.

A Drawing of Gertrude Paine

The third woman was referred to merely as Jane Doe.

Pennell's aim in filing the countersuit was to force Ed to drop the divorce suit through the threat of publicly shaming him. He was keenly aware that the March 5 divorce hearing date had already been set and that Ed had a strong case.

Alice agreed to the plan Arthur laid out and launched her countersuit. Incredibly, even after the amended complaint was filed, Alice continued to beg Ed to take her back.

In early February, Pennell demanded to meet with Ed again. He felt confident that the countersuit was a master stroke, and this time he was determined to stay on the offensive and in control of his emotions.

Ed agreed to the meeting, and Arthur came to his office and began to discuss Alice's countersuit in a cool, businesslike way. To his dismay, Ed was undeterred by the allegations, despite the possibility they contained an element of truth. Arthur revealed that detectives had followed Ed to Cleveland, Ohio, where he visited Mrs. Warren, and had observed him in Buffalo meeting with Mrs. Paine in different locations on a number of occasions.[x]

When his old friend seemed unimpressed by the countersuit, Pennell took a different tack. He said coolly that he could not accept any responsibility for Alice's "infatuation" with him. When Ed refused to take the bait, Arthur left.

Ed got to his feet. It was the end of the day, and he was exhausted. As he pulled on his coat, he confided to Parke that he blamed Pennell more than Alice for the affair.

Parke eyed his friend coolly. "Why don't you kill him?" he asked.

Ed looked shocked. "How can I care for my children with a murder on my hands?"

Parke shrugged and told his business partner to look out for Pennell.

Burdick waved away the warning. Pennell was a physical coward, he said. He had no fear of him. Parke looked after him curiously, remembering the day Ed told him he feared for his life. He was sure that his friend was truly afraid of someone, and he knew that Burdick kept his new revolver on his person at all times. If he wasn't afraid of Pennell, who did he fear?

The Burdicks' marital woes were well-known to the Elmwood Avenue set, of course, and as divorce suit details leaked out, an ethical question arose. Was it right, they mused, for Arthur Pennell to represent Alice, given that his affair with her had destroyed the Burdicks' marriage in the first place?

Before a consensus could be reached, something horrific happened.

Part 2

Something Wicked

Thursday, February 26, was, in almost every sense, an ordinary day for Ed. He had worked all morning and partway through the afternoon. At three o'clock, a friend from the Red Jacket Golf Club stopped by his office to discuss the upcoming election of officers. Afterward, Ed had a business appointment on Niagara Street.

Only two things marked his day as unusual. The first was that on his way home from work, he stopped to buy a bottle of premixed cocktails. Ed drank only socially and never purchased cocktails for himself. The second was his awareness that less than a week from that day, his marriage to Alice would officially be over.

Edwin Burdick seemed to be at peace with the end of his marriage. Just over a year ago, he had written a bitter letter to Alice. At the time, he was still deeply hurt but he had attempted to disguise his pain by pretending to be scornful of her:

> *You have created a situation, or allowed yourself to be placed in one, where it is possible for one person only to extricate you, and he refuses. I am sorry for you now, but I hope the future has great happiness in store for you and I will contribute all I can, consistently, to your happiness. I forgive you the wrong you have done me, and ask forgiveness for my own numerous shortcomings. I am sorry you are not well but believe you will be better now that Pennell has settled your future for you.*

Now, with the divorce just days away, he meant the words he had written then.

As the months passed and Alice continued to treat him poorly, Ed's pretended contempt toward his wife had given way to the real thing. He had done all he could to save their marriage, for the sake of his children and his desire to avoid scandal. However, the past three months had wrought a change in Ed, and he now saw that he could have never been happy with Alice again. He felt a real sense of relief that she had made such a reconciliation impossible and now that her future was no longer entwined with his, he sincerely wished her well. What he saw when he looked into his future is unknown.

Ed arrived at home on Thursday evening at about 6:30 p.m. as the cook cleared the table, the family retired to the back parlor. When they had company, the Burdicks always entertained their guests in the formal front parlor, with its new, modern furniture and décor. However, if the family was alone, they preferred to spend the evenings in the large, informal back parlor with its sagging sofa and worn chairs.

Ed played with the children, and he and Marion discussed the possibility of adopting a puppy until Mrs. Hull summoned her eldest granddaughter to do her homework. At 9:30 p.m., she put the girls to bed and retired to her room. She changed into her nightgown and read for 20 minutes, according to her habit.

About 9:45 p.m., she heard Ed's familiar step in the hall. He could see the dim light emanating from the strip beneath her doorway. As he passed, he murmured, "Good night, Mother Hull."

Mrs. Hull responded with a civil, "Good night, Edwin." She locked her bedroom door, a habit she had adopted when she was a young girl. Generally, one of her granddaughters slept in her room, but that night she was alone. She removed her gold-rimmed glasses and turned down the gaslight.

Mrs. Hull, Ed's mother-in-law

About 30 minutes later, a key turned in the lock of the back door. Maggie Murray, the Burdicks' cook, entered the house, shivering. It was a cold night with temperatures reaching only 20 degrees. Maggie was grateful it had stopped snowing.

She locked the door and yawned. It had been an unusually late evening for her. She was an early riser and was typically asleep at this time.

Maggie locked the door behind her and stepped into the hall, noticing with surprise that the door to Mr. Burdick's den was open and the room was well lit. Ed emerged a moment later, as if investigating a noise. As soon as he saw her, Ed moved back into the den and partially closed the door.

Maggie blushed. Mr. Burdick was a formal man, and she had clearly caught him unawares, for he was clad only in his underwear. She wondered, as she climbed the stairs to her room, whether her employer always went to his den later in the evening.

Maggie washed her face, changed into her nightgown quickly, and entered the room she shared with Katie Koenig, who worked as a maid for the Burdicks. The room was silent except for Katie's deep, even breathing, and Maggie soon felt herself drifting off. The last noise she heard before sleep overtook her was the distant, familiar sound of someone filling the furnace with coal.

The next morning, Maggie awoke at approximately 6:45 a.m., without the aid of an alarm clock. In the feeble morning light, she readied herself for the day. She shivered as she descended the steps and wondered why the house was so cold.

She stopped in surprise near the foot of the stairs. The front door was standing open. She crossed the foyer and stood in the doorway looking outside, but not a soul was in sight.

Maggie frowned. She had lived with and worked for the Burdick family for two years, and never before had she awakened to find the front door open. Typically, Mr. Burdick locked the front and back doors at night.

Shaking off her nervousness, she shut the door firmly and proceeded to the kitchen. But as she walked into the kitchen, she immediately noticed the window was open as well.

Thieves, she thought. She darted out of the kitchen and up the stairs. She paused in front of her employer's closed bedroom door.

Katie was sorting the laundry in the hallway, and she looked at Maggie reproachfully. "It's only just seven o'clock," she said, with a frown. "Mr. Burdick isn't up yet."

Maggie told her about the open door and window. Katie's eyes widened, and Maggie turned and tapped on her employer's bedroom door. "Mr. Burdick, sir, it's Maggie. There's thieves been in the house, sir."

After debating a moment, Maggie turned the door knob and opened the door a crack. "Mr. Burdick, sir?" When the silence persisted, the cook adjusted her apron self-consciously and stepped inside. The curtains were closed, but the gaslight on the wall was still flickering. It took a moment for her eyes to adjust to the darkness.

When she was able to make out the room, Maggie blinked at the empty bed. "Katie!" she hissed.

Katie hurried into the room and stared at the empty bed. "He never slept here last night," she said wonderingly. "The bed is just how I made it up!"

Then Maggie remembered she had seen her employer downstairs late the night before. A vague feeling of dread filled her. "I seen Mr. Burdick in his den last night," she told Katie. "He must have fell asleep down there. I suppose I'll wake him."

Muffled noises across the hall galvanized them. "Go put some coal in the furnace, Katie," Maggie urged. She nodded at Mrs. Hull's closed door. "You can see your breath in the downstairs hallway, and she'll squawk if it isn't fixed."

Katie immediately hurried down the back steps to the cellar, while Maggie walked slowly down the front steps. The door to the den was closed. She hesitated in front of it, twisting her hands, but she could not summon the courage to open it, or even to knock. She felt certain something wicked waited behind that door. After a moment, she turned and rushed back upstairs and tapped lightly on Mrs. Hull's bedroom door.

Mrs. Hull opened the door and displayed no surprise at the sight of the cook, breathlessly pouring out her story. She listened silently, and when Maggie stopped speaking, she told her to go downstairs and see to breakfast. "I expect we'll be ready by 8:30, as usual," Mrs. Hull informed her. "I'll look for Mr. Burdick."

Maggie looked at her in confusion. "Yes, ma'am."

Mrs. Hull waited until Maggie's steps had faded away, then she crossed the hallway and opened the door to her son-in-law's bedroom. As Maggie had said, the bed was still made from the day before; Ed had not slept in his room. He was very regular in his habits, and it would be unlike him to fall asleep anywhere other than his bedroom.

Mrs. Hull turned down the gaslight before returning to the hall and shutting the door firmly behind her. She found Maggie waiting at the bottom of the front stairs for her. "Breakfast will be ready on time, ma'am," she said.

Mrs. Hull nodded. "I am looking for Mr. Burdick," she said. She walked past the cook, as if to go into the den, but she stopped in front of the closed door, as if she was stopped by the same strange force that had arrested Maggie. She whispered, "I am frightened!"

The cook watched as Mrs. Hull rapped loudly on the door. After listening in vain for a response, she turned the knob and gave the door a push. It swung open. The shades were drawn, and the room was in total darkness. Gradually Mrs. Hull could discern a shape on the long Turkish divan.

"Maggie, I don't dare to go in there. Will you go in and see what—whatever is there?" Mrs. Hull's steely blue eyes peered at her intently.

Maggie shook her head violently. "Mrs. Hull, no, ma'am! I would not go in there for the world."

Mrs. Hull turned back to look into the darkened den. She suddenly cried out, "Ed! Ed!" When no answer came, she nearly screamed, "Ed!".

Still, no one responded. Mrs. Hull whispered, "I fear something dreadful has happened. Someone is under those pillows. I do not dare go in there!" She pulled the door shut again.

The next step was to call for Dr. Marcy, the Burdicks' family physician, and Maggie moved toward the house telephone. "No." Mrs. Hull's voice stopped her. "Put breakfast on the table. When you are done, go and telephone from Smither & Thurstone's drug store." Seeing the question on Maggie's face, she explained, "I don't wish the girls to hear anything."

Twenty minutes later, the telephone rang at the home of Dr. Marcy. In a breathless voice, Maggie Murray introduced herself and said something was wrong with Mr. Burdick. Could the doctor please come at once? The doctor tried to question her, but Maggie was already gone.

Meanwhile, Mrs. Hull went upstairs to ensure her granddaughters were awake and preparing for school. She paused in the doorway of her bedroom for a moment.

"What's wrong?" a young voice asked. Mrs. Hull turned to see Marion standing in her doorway, clutching her schoolbooks.

Mrs. Hull heaved a sigh. "I'm afraid your father is very ill."

Startled, the girl asked, "Where is he, Grandma?"

"He's in his den," Mrs. Hull replied. [xi] "Come down for breakfast, Marion."

The girl asked no more questions but walked downstairs obediently. She put her books on a chair in the foyer and passed the closed door of the den on her way to the dining room.

While the family ate breakfast, Dr. William H. Marcy raced over, unsure of what to expect. He could not imagine what was wrong with Ed. Dr. Marcy had been the family physician for seven years and had visited the Burdicks in January. He had talked with Ed at the time, and he appeared to be perfectly healthy.

Dr. Marcy arrived a few minutes after nine o'clock. Mrs. Hull opened the door before he could ring; she had evidently been waiting for him. As he struggled to remove his overcoat, she told him how Maggie had found the door and window open that morning then discovered Ed had not slept in his room.

"I came to the door of the den and called to him, but he did not answer," Mrs. Hull added. "I believe he must be ill."

The doctor put his hand on the doorknob. "Why don't you wait out here, Mrs. Hull?" he suggested kindly. "I'll come back in a few moments and let you know about the state of things."

Mrs. Hull stepped back and watched as Dr. Marcy stepped into the den, and closed the door behind him.

The doctor advanced slowly into the den, holding his hands out in front of him to feel his way along in the inky darkness. Despite his caution, he bumped into an unseen object that caused him to stumble a few feet toward the windows. He fumbled with the Venetian blinds, pulled too hard, and the rod slipped, causing the blinds to tumble down.

Feeble sunlight flooded the den. He turned back to the room and beheld a sight like none he had ever encountered—and one he hoped he would never again see. Something horrible had happened in this room. He slowly approached the sofa, noting the blood on the floor and the walls. He could see what appeared to be a man's naked body, covered by several pillows and rugs.

Dr. Marcy pulled away a couple of the pillows. The body lie facedown, wearing only an undershirt that had ridden up near the ribs. The head was covered, wrapped in a log cabin quilt. It was evident the man was dead, but Dr. Marcy searched for a pulse anyway. There was none.

The doctor was sure the body belonged to Ed. It was his den, after all, and the body on the sofa was about 5'6" and slight, which matched Burdick's height and build. Before the doctor would tell Burdick's family he was dead, however, he had to be sure beyond any doubt that it really was Ed. Marcy carefully unwound the quilt, just enough to see the face.

Ed Burdick's last formal photograph, circa 1902

He drew in his breath sharply. Indeed, it was Ed, and he had met a violent end. Any queasiness Dr. Marcy had ever felt at the sight of death had disappeared years ago. He had seen many murders over the course of his career, but they had been committed with firearms or knives.

This was different. The gentle, mild-mannered Ed Burdick had been bludgeoned to death with some object. And whoever killed him had not been satisfied with merely ending his life. A blow, or perhaps two, likely would have killed Burdick. But the body on the sofa had been hit over and over, at least a dozen times. The doctor rewound the quilt over the crushed skull, attempting to make it look as it had when he had found it.

He picked his way back across the room, opened the door, and stepped out. Mrs. Hull was waiting for him in the hall. Her cold blue eyes studied him. "Well, doctor?"

The doctor looked at her grimly and said, "Madam, I regret to tell you that Mr. Burdick is deceased. He's been murdered."

If Dr. Marcy expected an emotional reaction, he was disappointed. Mrs. Hull merely stated that she needed to inform the girls. "I'll be back momentarily, Dr. Marcy." The doctor bowed his assent.

He watched as Mrs. Hull walked into the dining room. He could see the three girls sitting at the table, and they looked up when she entered. He heard her announce, "Children, your father is dead."

Dr. Marcy, not wanting to intrude, stepped away to telephone the medical examiner, Dr. John Howland, and asked him to come to 101 Ashland Avenue. It would be up to Howland to establish the cause of Mr. Burdick's death and the time it occurred.

Maggie had overheard Mrs. Hull's announcement to the girls. She quickly sought out Katie and repeated the dreadful news in a whisper. The two women huddled in the kitchen in a state of shock.

"It must have been a heart attack," Katie insisted. "He wasn't sick. I know he wasn't sick."

"No," Maggie told her. "Some burglar's come in here and murdered him. Why else would the door and the window be open?"

"Who would kill Mr. Burdick?" the maid protested.

They were so engrossed in their conversation, Maggie lost track of time. With a start, she looked up at the clock and saw it was nearly 10:00 a.m. She hurried into the dining room and rapidly cleared the table. She had just finished washing the dishes when Dr. Marcy called to her.

Maggie nervously wiped her hands on her apron and hurried into the hallway, where the doctor and Mrs. Hull were standing. "Sir?"

"Take Mrs. Hull to the kitchen and fix her some tea," he said. "She's had a bad shock. I'll trust you to take care of her."

"Yes, sir." Maggie's forehead relaxed. "Come with me, ma'am. I'll have a nice cup of hot tea for you in just a moment."

Mrs. Hull nodded. "You will remember to notify Mr. Parke, doctor?"

Dr. Marcy said he would. It was strange that it should fall to him to inform Ed's business partner of his death, but he didn't want to put the extra strain on Mrs. Hull.

Medical Examiner Howland arrived at 10:15 a.m. Dr. Marcy pulled open the heavy front door and ushered him into the house. John Howland was a quiet man who was well-regarded in his field, especially for a man under 40 years of age. Howland took his hat off and greeted Dr. Marcy politely.

Marcy returned the greeting soberly and took Howland's overcoat before adding, "My patient, Ed Burdick, has died."

"What happened?"

"Eh, let's have a word together," Marcy said. He looked around quickly, then satisfied no one was listening, asked in a low voice, "Are you aware that Mr. Burdick was having marital difficulties?"

The medical examiner shook his head, looking bewildered.

Dr. Marcy explained the Burdicks' divorce would have been finalized the following week. "And—well, to be frank with you, there are rumors about Mrs. Burdick's conduct. The family has had all they can do to try to muffle the scandal, and if it were to get abroad that a murder was done on account of—of anything—whether relating to those difficulties or no ... well, it would not do."

Howland's eyebrows shot up. "A murder?"

"I'd like to save the family any more scandal," Dr. Marcy sighed. "I don't tell you what to find, you understand. All I say is, if it looks like a suicide to you, why, I'm very glad to have it look so. If possible, I'd like for you to make it out a suicide in your report."

"And if it doesn't look like a suicide?" Howland asked, with a small smile.

"If it does not, I am sorry. I hope it will." Marcy rose abruptly. "Let us go to the den, and you can see for yourself."

Howland stood up as Dr. Marcy marched across the hall and opened the den door. "The body is in here, on the divan." He stood back to allow Howland to pass.

Dr. Howland walked to the body while Marcy stayed by the door. Instantly, the medical examiner knew something was amiss in the way Dr. Marcy had presented the case. For a moment, he stood looking down at the body. Ed was lying on his stomach, and though the head was wrapped in a blanket, Howland could tell by the way the neck was turned that his face was pointed outward toward the room.

Frowning, Howland stooped down and gingerly unwound the blanket. Ed Burdick's skull was destroyed, crushed by repeated blows. Glancing up, the medical examiner saw the pillows, quilt, and the walls near the divan were streaked with blood and brain matter. A pool of blood had soaked through the quilt and the sofa cushions, creating a little puddle drying beneath the divan.

Howland studied the body for several seconds in silence, then he turned to face the doctor. One needed no medical training whatsoever to see the battered body on the divan was the victim of a homicide—and a vicious homicide, at that.

"Dr. Marcy," he said severely. "*No one* would entertain the idea of a suicide."

Marcy saw instantly in the medical examiner's demeanor that there was no point in pleading his case. His mouth hardened beneath his heavy moustache. "Well, I'd hoped you could, but if you cannot, you cannot."

Howland exhaled. "No, I cannot." Without waiting for further comment, he stepped into the hall where he spotted a woman, whom he took to be a servant. She showed him where the telephone was, and he called the police to report a homicide at 101 Ashland Avenue.

John Howland was confident he had made the right decision, but Dr. Marcy's request to classify Ed's death as a suicide disturbed him. He imagined the case was likely one in which the cause of death was unclear. It distressed him to realize the doctor was attempting to influence him to falsify the manner of death. The medical examiner valued integrity and he was shocked by what he viewed as utter lack of judgement.

A few minutes later, he returned to the den to examine the body in more detail. When he entered, Dr. Marcy said, "I'll leave you here. Mr. Parke, Mr.

Burdick's business partner, will be here momentarily, and I need to give him the news."

"Just one thing, Dr. Marcy," Howland said quickly. Dr. Marcy paused on the threshold. "Did you find the head wrapped up in this way?"

"I did," Dr. Marcy replied. Finding the medical examiner had no other questions, he left the den, closing the door silently behind him.

Detectives Holmlund and Sullivan arrived about 10:30 a.m., followed closely by Ed's business partner, Charles Parke. As Dr. Howland greeted the police, Dr. Marcy took Parke aside.

Once they were out of earshot, Dr. Marcy said sympathetically, "It's been a bit of a shock to you."

Parke shook his head in bewilderment and spoke faintly. "Dr. Marcy, I feel I must not have understood you when you telephoned. Is Ed really dead? What has happened?"

"Yes," Dr. Marcy replied. "Someone has murdered Mr. Burdick."

Parke stopped in the act of removing his heavy coat. "Murdered him! Ed was murdered?"

"Yes, he's been murdered," Marcy muttered. "I tried to make it out as suicide, but it would not do."

Parke looked at him blankly. "But why?"

Before either man could speak again, a voice behind them demanded, "Yes, why? How could anybody have the heart to kill Ed?"

Both men jumped and turned to look at Mrs. Hull, who stood a few feet away from them. She continued, "For that matter, why would someone rob these children of their father?" She removed her glasses and dabbed at her eyes.

"Mrs. Hull, you must remember your heart, ma'am," Dr. Marcy said sternly. "I insist you lie down. We cannot let anything happen to you when the children will be relying on you so much."

Without waiting for her response, the doctor escorted her out of the room. After a brief introduction to the police detectives and Dr. Howland, Marcy again insisted that she go to her room and rest. He left her on the threshold and assured her he would not allow her to be disturbed.

The Savage Murder of Ed Burdick

Police Chief Patrick Cusack was the last policeman to arrive. Cusack was 64 years old and had been with the police department for twenty years, slowly working his way up. He had an observant, sharp eye, but his easy demeanor could disarm even the most hard-boiled character. He was well-liked by the other officers and especially his detectives.

After disposing of his coat and hat, Chief Cusack asked to see the body. He stepped over the threshold into the den and took a moment to take in his surroundings. According to contemporaneous accounts, "the den was located on the north side of the house on the first floor and it was accessible by a door connecting it with the front hall and reception room. That was the only door. Two windows faced the north, which were closed in by slatted shutters." XII

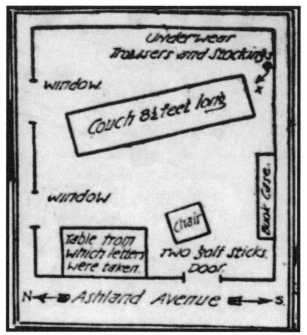

A diagram of the den, based on police notes

The den was a large room, sparsely but comfortably furnished. A bookcase covered much of one wall, and there was an oversized leather chair, a table, and a large Turkish divan. Two golf clubs leaned against the wall near the door. The divan was piled high with rugs and pillows that would normally have been scattered about the room to create a more inviting look.

Burdick had a large table, with a single shallow drawer, which he used as a writing desk. The drawer was open and a number of papers, photographs, and other small items lay scattered on the floor in that vicinity. Cusack made a mental note to look into this. For now, he wanted to hear from the medical examiner.

"Now, Dr. Howland," Cusack began. "Before we begin our investigation, suppose you tell us your findings." He pulled a small notebook and a sharpened pencil from his vest pocket.

"Of course," Howland replied. He told the police chief that Ed had been beaten to death, estimating the time of death to be roughly 2:00 a.m.

He partially unwrapped the quilt to expose Ed's skull. "The first blow was to the back of the head, and probably caught the victim unawares. It likely would have killed him within a minute or two, but if you see here–" he picked up Burdick's left hand "two of his left fingers are broken. He must have put up a hand to try to protect himself, and the fingers were broken in the second strike."

"He was hit more than two times, it looks like," Detective Sullivan observed.

"Yes, certainly," Howland agreed. "There were a number of subsequent blows, as the autopsy would doubtless show. You see the victim's skull has been pulverized."

"The body was moved after the murder was done." Howland pointed out a small spot of dried blood about 15 inches away, toward the end of the divan. "He initially fell there, but the murderer pulled him further down. It made his shirt ride up, as it is now. And look here." Their eyes followed his pointing finger to a bloody thumbprint on one of Burdick's calves.

"Dr. Marcy may have additional insight," he added. "The family called him first and he was the first person to see the body."

"We'll talk with him shortly," Cusack said. "Do we have the murder weapon?"

"I've not seen it. I only looked in the immediate vicinity though," Howland admitted. "It would have been a heavy, blunt object. Possibly a fire poker, or something along those lines."

"Perhaps a golf club?" Chief Cusack suggested, nodding toward the two clubs against the wall.

The medical examiner's eyes traveled in the direction the chief indicated. He nodded in agreement. "Either of those clubs would answer."

Detective Sullivan crouched next to the clubs and examined them closely. "Not a speck of blood on either of them." He picked up one of the clubs. "They are lightweight, though. This is only two pounds, I'd estimate."

"It could do the job," Howland said quietly. "It's not just the weight of the instrument. There's also the velocity, the force with which it was swung."

The police chief eyed Howland. He was a quiet man but sharp and a keen observer. Often, the medical men had a unique perspective on a crime that was helpful to consider. "What do you make of all of this, sir?" he asked. "What do you think happened here?"

The medical examiner looked surprised. "I am only qualified to speak to the condition of the body."

"Of course," Cusack replied. "I ask informally."

Howland glanced around the room and then back at the body. "The scene here, in this room, tells us Burdick was in here with a woman, and they perhaps quarreled. She killed him and arranged things as we see them now. But—I don't believe that a woman did this."

"Go on."

"Well, look here," Howland said. He again unwrapped the quilt, and pointed to the deep wounds on Ed's head. "There is the sheer physicality of the crime. As the detective here says, it would take a certain amount of physical strength to cause these wounds," he explained, as though he were lecturing to a room of medical students. "That would be the case, no matter what the weapon was."

"Strength that a woman could not possess?"

The young doctor frowned slightly as he replaced the quilt. "In my experience with homicides, woman do not kill violently. How many times was the victim struck? At least ten, maybe 20. The killer was in a rage he could not control. If a woman wishes to put a man out of the way, she chooses a clean, quiet method. A bit of poison in his tea or some such thing."

"Yes, that is true." Cusack nodded approvingly. "You mention that it looks as though Burdick was entertaining a woman. Is Mrs. Burdick deceased?"

"No, sir," Dr. Howland replied. "My understanding is that Mrs. Burdick is in Atlantic City, and that she and Burdick are in the process of divorcing."

Cusack stopped scribbling and looked up. "Are they now?" he murmured curiously. "For what reason, I wonder?"

"Dr. Marcy mentioned there had been gossip about Mrs. Burdick's behavior," Howland replied. "I don't know the details."

The detectives exchanged glances with Chief Cusack. If another man was involved in the Burdick's troubles, he would be the logical person to investigate. "Was a corespondent named in the divorce?"

"I've no idea."

Cusack thanked Howland and allowed him to go.

Three Perspectives

The detectives were setting up a tripod. Crime scene photography was a new innovation for the police department, and photographing the body would take some time. Afterward, they would go through the den seeking clues.

Chief Cusack left the room to interview the occupants of the house. The first person he met, however, was Dr. Marcy. "May I ask you a few questions in private, sir?" the chief asked. The doctor agreed and followed Cusack to a vacant room, evidently used by the Burdicks as a formal parlor.

Dr. Marcy could add little information to what the chief had already been told. Cusack was struck by the doctor's hope, expressed repeatedly, that the matter could be settled as quietly as possible, for the sake of the family.

"The murder, I think, would be more traumatic than whatever might be said of it," the chief ventured.

"The murder is terrible enough," the doctor agreed. "But the family has suffered from the scandal stemming from Mr. Burdick's divorce suit. People talk, you know."

"People do talk, but for the family to lose Mr. Burdick—"

"Of course, it's a tragedy," Dr. Marcy cut him off. "Of course it is. But you must think of the girls. They're very young, and with this coming on top of the scandal of a divorce, you know it affects them in many ways. The people who associate with them, their eventual marriage prospects, everything."

Cusack nodded. He thought it was unusual for the doctor to be preoccupied with the eventual marriage prospects of the Burdick children rather than the violent murder of his patient, but he pushed the thought out of his mind.

He asked about events that morning, and the doctor told him that he had gone into the den, and upon discovering Burdick's body, notified Mrs. Hull. She had then told the children of their father's death while he called Dr. Howland. He knew nothing more.

Maggie entered the room with a broom and a dustpan and started when she saw them. "I didn't know anyone was here," she apologized. "I'll do this later."

Cusack held up a hand to stop her. "Just a moment, Miss—"

"Margaret Murray," the house maid supplied. "Maggie."

"Maggie, Dr. Marcy and I were just finished. May I speak to you for a few moments?"

Maggie Murray, the Burdick's cook.

The young woman sat down. She had gotten hold of herself since the early morning hours when her employer's body was found and was beginning to find the events to be rather exciting.

The chief adopted a slightly different demeanor with Maggie than he had with Dr. Marcy. The hardness disappeared from his voice, replaced by a more chatty, friendly approach. His Irish brogue had been softened by 20 years in the United States, but as he talked with Maggie, it became prominent. His intuition proved correct. The young woman became more communicative, but whether her information was of real importance, Cusack couldn't yet determine.

According to Maggie, Ed Burdick enjoyed socializing but was not given to heavy drinking or other vices. Burdick never raised his voice in anger, nor was he unreasonable. He did believe in propriety and insisted that if she were going out for the evening, she must return by 10:30 p.m.

"And were you back by 10:30 last night, Maggie?"

"I looked at the kitchen clock before I even took my coat off," Maggie replied. "It was 10:18 exactly."

"And did you see Mr. Burdick after you came in?"

Maggie said she encountered Ed in front of the den, but when he caught sight of her, he stepped back in and closed the door partway.

"Did you see anyone in there with him? Or hear them talking?"

"No, sir," Maggie said. "Mr. Burdick was alone."

The chief raised an eyebrow. "Well, you didn't *see* anybody. But that doesn't mean nobody was there. He closed the door, didn't he?"

"He just shut it about halfway. If it was a private conversation, he would have shut the door." After a moment, Maggie added, "There weren't no voices. I'm sure he was alone."

"He didn't speak to you?"

"No, sir. He stepped back real quick when he seen it was me. He was only wearing his underclothes, and I guess he was embarrassed I seen him."

Cusack smothered a smile and asked if she had noticed anything else. Maggie said that about 20 minutes after she reached her bedroom, she heard Mr. Burdick putting more coal in the furnace.

"He must've been awfully loud down in the cellar if you heard him on the third floor."

Maggie shook her head. "He wasn't loud. It's just the way the house is. You can hear noises from the cellar quite plain on the third floor, even though you can't on the first floor."

"Would you have been able to hear Mr. Burdick talking on the first floor up in your room?"

Maggie thought for a moment. "Not unless he was talking loud, but Mr. Burdick never shouts. It's the house noises that you can hear. Like if someone puts coal in the furnace, or when the doors open."

"And you didn't hear any voices after that?"

Maggie shook her head. "No, sir. It was late, and nobody was here. The first visitor we had was Dr. Marcy this morning. Or perhaps Alfred."

"Alfred who?" Cusack asked sharply.

"I don't know Alfred who," Maggie replied petulantly. "His name is Alfred, and he sees to the furnace. Katie seen him this morning and asked him to come in and put more coal on since Mr. Burdick was sick." Maggie estimated Alfred arrived sometime after 9:15 a.m.

"Did Mr. Burdick ever have visitors?"

"Sure, people would come to talk with him about business or that golfing club. He was the president, you know." Maggie was sure she had never witnessed any unpleasantness between Mr. Burdick and anyone who called on him.

"Did any ladies call on him socially?"

"The Paines sometimes come by. The dentist and his wife. Mrs. Warren come with them now and then." Maggie didn't know Mrs. Warren's first name or where she lived.

"But no ladies called on him alone?"

"Not that I know of."

The chief detected a hint of defensiveness in Maggie's tone. "Well, it wouldn't be so strange if he did have a lady visitor, would it?" he asked artfully. "I understand Mr. and Mrs. Burdick were going to be divorced."

"Yes," Maggie said. Cusack waited and she added reluctantly, "I knew they was getting a divorce, but I don't know what was the matter between them. I never heard them quarrel."

"Was Mr. Burdick downhearted about Mrs. Burdick leaving?"

"I don't think so," the cook replied. She thought for a moment and added, "When Mrs. Burdick was home, he seemed out of sorts. After she left in December, he seemed to sort of relax."

Chief Cusack could see there was little more he would learn from Maggie about the Burdick marriage. "Now, tell me all about what happened this morning."

Maggie described finding the front door and the window standing open. "I run upstairs to tell Mr. Burdick, but he wasn't in his room. Hadn't slept in his bed."

"Did you tell anyone what you'd found?"

"Well, I went down to the den first, sir," Maggie said. "I remembered Mr. Burdick was down there and thought maybe he'd fell asleep reading. Only when I got there, something stopped me from opening the door."

Cusack leaned forward. "Something was blocking the door?"

Maggie looked troubled. "No. I don't know what it was. Some bad feeling… there was something evil there."

"Oh-h, I see," Cusack said softly. "Go on."

Maggie said she had gone to Mrs. Hull's bedroom next. After explaining that Mrs. Hull was the children's grandmother, she went on. "I knocked and she come to the door. I told her what I found and she come down after a few minutes, and we stood by the door to the den. She was afraid to go in."

The police chief thought for a moment. "Did Mrs. Hull go into the den?"

"No sir," Maggie replied.

"Well, I imagine it was frightening for her, too," Cusack mused. "Imagine waking up from a dead sleep to find burglars have been in the house and your son-in-law is missing."

Maggie grimaced. "Nobody woke her up. Mrs. Hull gets up early every morning. She was already up and dressed when I came to her door."

"And how is Mrs. Hull to work for, I wonder?"

Maggie sniffed. "Oh, I like her fine."

"Is that right?" the chief asked. "I might be a bit prejudiced, you know. I've always heard a person with a square jaw can be a wee bit challenging to live with. But I only just had a glimpse of her before the doctor shooed her upstairs."

The young woman gave him an expressive look. "You wouldn't believe it, were I to tell you. She runs things around here like a general on a forced march."

Cusack laughed. "Thank you, Maggie. I won't keep you any longer."

The chief next spoke to Charles Parke, Burdick's business partner. He found him in the kitchen, in a quiet conference with Dr. Marcy, and asked if he might have a word. Parke agreed at once and followed the chief into the parlor.

Parke said he was 40 years old, married, and that he and Burdick had been partners for about five years. He seemed to be in shock over the death of his friend.

"You must have been surprised to learn of his murder?"

"Indeed, I was," Parke said eagerly. "I was only told of his death over the telephone. It was not until I arrived here that Dr. Marcy told me it was a murder. I can scarcely believe it."

Cusack paused. "Were you less surprised when you thought it was a natural death? Was Burdick in poor health?"

Chief Patrick V. Cusack

"Oh no," Parke said. "But I would not have been entirely surprised if he had committed suicide."

The chief was careful to maintain his noncommittal expression. "Did Burdick express an intent to take his own life? Or had he made a prior attempt?"

Parke shook his head. "Not that I know of. And he isn't the sort who would do it, in general. But you know, he had his troubles. With his marriage, I mean."

Detective Sullivan knocked at the door. "We're finished in the den, Chief."

Cusack looked up in irritation. "That's all right. I'll be out after I'm done speaking with Mr. Parke. You fellows look around for anything the assailant might have dropped. Check the kitchen, the outside areas, and the cellar. The maid heard someone in the cellar last night. I imagine it was Burdick, but see if there's anything to be found."

As the detective turned to go, Cusack called after him. "One of you stay in the den and make sure no one goes in there. I want a look before anything is moved."

He turned back to Parke. "Now, you were saying Mr. Burdick was despondent over his divorce?"

Parke frowned. Ed was not despondent, he said, but eager for the divorce to be finalized.

Cusack raised his brows. "Mr. Burdick was not dreading the divorce?"

The businessman hastened to clarify, explaining that Ed's wife was having an affair with Arthur Pennell, a local attorney. "It had gone on so long, and it just wore away at Ed. He wanted to put it behind him but he did feel badly— primarily for what the divorce would mean for his children, I think."

"And did Burdick—well, to put it bluntly, did he have someone else in mind?"

Parke shrugged and said he didn't know. "You understand Ed didn't discuss personal matters often. I knew more about his marital troubles only because Pennell came to see him at the office recently. Occasionally, he received letters about it and he might make a comment in frustration."

"Do you know of anyone who wanted to harm Burdick?"

"Well, Mr. Pennell did. He threatened to kill Burdick when he came to the office. I heard it with my own ears."

"Threatened to kill him?" Cusack repeated. "What did he say, exactly?"

"Mr. Pennell wanted him to take his wife back again. Ed had sent her away, you know. Mr. Pennell said if Ed wouldn't end the divorce suit and take his wife back, he would kill Ed, Mrs. Burdick, and himself, too."

Parke appeared lost in thought. After a few moments he said, "*I* never thought Pennell was harmless. If a man threatens your life, I take him at his word. I told Ed to watch out for him more than once but he said—"

Cusack leaned forward. "Yes? What did he say?"

Parke frowned. "He said he took it for a bluff. "

The chief nodded. "And so, he took no steps to protect himself."

"No, that's not so," Parke said at once. "Ed got a revolver back in December and he had it with him always. He told me he feared for his life. But he told me that he didn't think Pennell could or would hurt him."

"What was the gun for, then?" Cusack demanded. "Did Burdick think another person was going to kill him?"

Parke shook his head. "I didn't ask him. I didn't like to pry into his personal business."

Cusack's mind was beginning to race. "You say you overheard all of this. Do you think Pennell's threats were serious? Would he have carried them out?"

"Oh yes," Parke said. "I think he's behind this. That's just my own idea, mind."

Cusack waited a moment before asking. "Why do you think it was Pennell who murdered Mr. Burdick?"

"Pennell, or someone he hired, perhaps," Parke added. "I just don't know of anyone else who would want to hurt Ed."

The chief was frowning. "And you say Mr. Pennell did not want Mrs. Burdick to get divorced."

Parke shrugged. "I only know what I heard him say. Mr. Pennell is married too, but I think it was the disclosures that would come out during the divorce suit that bothered him. He knew it would be very embarrassing for him."

"Ah, his wife would find him out?"

"Well no," Parke said. "His wife knew all about it."

Cusack looked up sharply. "How do you know that?"

"It was Mrs. Pennell who told Ed about the affair. And she wrote to him a few times at the office about it. Ed said that if she had just held her tongue to begin with, none of this would have happened."

"Wasn't Mrs. Pennell upset about the affair?"

"I don't know," Parke answered.

Cusack sat back and eyed Parke. "You know, I'm not in your circle, but from what you tell me, I rather think Burdick was the one with a motive for murder."

Parke nodded sympathetically. "Yes. That's just what I think, too. And it did bother Ed a lot, the way Mr. Pennell had come into their lives and then broken up his home. He was Ed's friend first, before all this happened with Mrs. Burdick."

"Pennell and Burdick were friends?" Cusack looked interested.

"Yes, the Pennells are part of the same social group, and they belonged to the Elmwood Dancing Club and the same golf club as Ed. They were good friends for a couple of years."

"Would Mr. Pennell have possibly had a key to the place?"

"I don't know." Parke was quiet a moment, then he added hesitantly, "There is one other thing that perhaps I should tell you."

"Yes?" Cusack watched the face of the other man intently.

"Ed knew much more about the affair than he told me, of course." Parke looked embarrassed. "He'd found some letters—I don't know where, but he found some letters Mr. Pennell had written to his wife, and copied them. I don't think she knew he'd seen them."

"Did he tell you what they contained?"

"No, just that they would be enough to secure a divorce. I do not know if that's important."

Cusack scratched a few notes. "Just one more thing, Mr. Parke. What are the living arrangements here? I understand Mrs. Burdick left in December."

Parke looked surprised. "I believe after Mrs. Burdick left, there was just Ed, the children, and Mrs. Hull. And some servants lived upstairs, but I don't know much about them."

"And Mrs. Hull is Mrs. Burdick's mother?"

Charles Parke confirmed this and added, "I believe she's been caring for the children since Mrs. Burdick left."

"Might've been awkward with Mrs. Hull living here after Mrs. Burdick left, eh?"

Parke considered. "I don't think it was. At least, Ed always spoke very respectfully about his mother-in-law. I remember he said once. 'Mrs. Hull has stood by me through all this trouble.' I think he appreciated her."

"Do you like her?"

"I never saw her before today, and I'm afraid I did not pay much attention to her," Parke replied. "She seemed very much affected, and Dr. Marcy insisted she rest."

Chief Cusack thanked Parke and got to his feet. He felt confident that Ed's business partner and Maggie Murray had told him all they knew. He was less confident about Dr. William Marcy. For now, he was eager to learn what his detectives had discovered.

A Conjuring Trick

The detectives were waiting for the chief in the hall. Cusack motioned them to return to the den with him.

In the course of duty, the police quickly became desensitized to the presence of death. The bloody crime scene and the presence of Ed's battered body in the den did not cause the detectives undue anxiety. Rather, it was a window of opportunity to reconstruct the crime.

The chief closed the door to the den and turned to face the Holmlund and Sullivan. "Well, gentlemen?"

Detective Holmlund, the senior police detective, spoke. "We've been able to discern much of what happened last night, sir." Ed Burdick had gone to his bedroom as usual, around 9:45 p.m. to change from his suit jacket and dress shoes into his smoking jacket and slippers.

"The jacket he had worn to work was on a chair in his bedroom, and his dress shoes were up there as well.

"He had a housecoat that he put on, and then a smoking jacket and slippers——they're over there by the sofa now." The detective gestured vaguely in the direction of the sofa. "This was in the pocket of the housecoat." Holmlund held up a small black revolver.

Cusack took it and opened the chamber. "Fully loaded," he commented. "Doesn't look like it's been fired."

"No, sir," the detective replied. "We wanted to find out from the family if he typically came back downstairs in the evening to his den or if he might have come down to investigate a noise. Sullivan and I tried at different times to talk to Mrs. Hull and the eldest daughter."

"You 'tried' to?" Cusack repeated skeptically.

"Well, the doctor—he didn't want us to ask questions, that was plain."

"Which doctor? Dr. Marcy?"

"Marcy, to be sure," Holmlund said. "If it was Mrs. Hull we wanted to talk to, he would answer the questions for her. I protested this, but he said he would answer for her, as Mrs. Hull has a weak heart."

"And Mrs. Hull?"

"Mrs. Hull seemed happy to let him answer."

"I wanted to ask Howland some questions too, but Marcy interrupted us so persistently, I decided to call on him later."

Cusack's eyes shifted. Dr. Marcy's behavior all morning had been questionable. "Well, back to the crime," he said aloud. "Maggie the cook told me she came in at approximately 10:15 last night," he told the detectives. "She surprised Burdick. He stepped out of the den in his underwear to see who was there. She thinks he was alone at that point."

The detectives absorbed this new information with puzzled expressions. After a moment, Holmlund continued. "There was no forced entry. Either Burdick recognized the person and let them in, or the murderer had gotten into the house some other way earlier."

"What about the open window in the kitchen?" Cusack asked.

"In all probability, it was opened after the murder," Holmlund replied. "It looks like an attempt to stage the scene. The snow on the window sill had been brushed off, as if someone had slid into the house that way. When we went outside to look, there were no footprints in the snow under the window nor for several feet around it. Nobody's walked over that way in a week or more. Whoever brushed the snow off did so from inside the house."

Cusack nodded grimly. "So, what is the theory, Holmlund?"

Holmlund looked at Sullivan then turned back to Cusack with a slight shrug. "We're operating under the theory that Burdick let the murderer in and talked to him, not realizing that person intended to do him harm. He prepared some refreshments—the tray is still where he left it." Detective Holmlund gestured to the table.

Cusack strode over and examined it. The tray held a plate with some crackers and half-eaten cheese, a cocktail glass, a six-ounce bottle of liquor, and the remnants of a tart.

"There's only one glass," Cusack pointed out. "How do we know it was for someone else? Perhaps Mr. Burdick intended to eat the food himself."

Holmlund shook his head. "We spoke to the cook. She made the tart herself. But she was sure Burdick would not have eaten it. She said he didn't like this type of food, and he never drank liquor. We spoke to Katie, the maid here, and she says he only smoked down here. Never ate or drank anything in the den."

Cusack held the glass up to the light. "The glass has been used," he remarked.

Holmlund cleared his throat. "It is our conclusion, chief, that after murdering Burdick, the killer staged the scene to make it look as though a stranger had broken in through the window, committed the crime, and then fled through the front door. We believe, however, that Burdick let him in the front door.

"At some point," the detective continued, "Burdick turned away from this person, facing the bookcase, or thereabouts. The murderer saw his chance. He seized a heavy object and got behind the victim while his back was turned and struck a terrific blow to his head."

Burdick would have fallen forward, dazed. It was rather incredible he was conscious at that point, but the broken fingers told them he indisputably was. He partially turned, holding up his left hand in a futile effort to ward off additional blows. His attacker struck at him repeatedly, in a frenzied attack, even after it was obvious Burdick was dead or dying.

Cusack recalled his conversation with Charles Parke. He said Burdick feared someone and the fact Ed brought his gun to the den seemed to confirm that. It was ridiculous for a man to have to arm himself to read in his den. And yet, the murder proved Burdick's instincts were correct.

Detective Holmlund then brought forward a critical piece of evidence. The detectives found a clump of hair on the victim's torso, perhaps 18 or 20 individual strands, and the roots were visible. The strands were similar in color to Burdick's hair, which could be described as ash brown or dark gray. "It's longer than most men would wear it," Holmlund said.

"Perhaps we should seriously consider, gentlemen, whether all of this is the handiwork of a woman," Cusack said slowly. "Dr. Howland thought not, and I admit I agreed with his assertion that this is not typical of the fairer sex. Yet we must admit it is at least possible that a woman did perpetrate this awful crime. And much of the evidence here suggests a woman."

"Could there not have been two perpetrators, a male and a female?" Detective Sullivan ventured. No one hazarded a guess, and the discussion returned to the motive behind the murder. The motive, they believed, would tell them the identity of the murderer– or murderers.

The detectives ruled out a common burglary right away. It wasn't a stranger who had broken in to take anything of value he could find. Several costly items in plain view in the den had not been disturbed and so far, no one had identified any missing property from the home. Also, Ed's trousers were part of the pile of clothing on the floor at the far end of the divan, and a wallet containing $40 was in the pocket.

The detectives considered the possibility that Ed had a midnight visitor who had gone temporarily insane and killed him, but they were skeptical. It was unlikely for many reasons, not the least of which was the missing murder weapon. If nothing was missing from the house and the murder weapon could not be ascertained, they could only conclude that Ed's killer brought the weapon with him and took it away again.

No, this was a planned murder. The killer must have had a tremendous fury in his heart, but he concealed it so well that even his appearance in the middle of the night caused Ed no alarm. His face must have been one Ed knew well, most likely that of a trusted friend. Who else would he have admitted into his home at that hour of the night?

Gertrude Paine's photograph was amongst Ed's possessions.

The detectives had found a picture of an attractive young woman under the desk. There was no inscription but Detective Sullivan recognized her. "That's Mrs. Paine, the dentist's wife," he informed Cusack. "She's in the society columns a good deal. My wife has pointed her out to me."

Holmlund picked up the wallet, and handed it to Cusack. "We found more evidence in here," he said. He pointed out a clipping from a Cleveland, Ohio, newspaper. It was a brief announcement that a divorce had been granted to Mrs. Helen Warren from her husband J. Burton Warren.

Cusack squinted at it. It was nearly two weeks old. "What is this?" he asked. "Did Burdick travel to Cleveland recently?"

"We'll be looking into that. We found some interesting clues in the wallet. It looks like Burdick had copies of another man's love letters to his wife."

"Arthur Pennell," Cusack muttered. He looked at the top one, which was addressed to *My dearest Alice*. He sighed and folded it, intending to read them later.

"Chief, if you'll look at the second paragraph on that top letter, we found the first sentence to be rather significant." Cusack unfolded the letter again and read: *When I think of how he has treated you, I feel I must kill Ed Burdick!*

"Well, well," he sighed. "Between this and what Burdick's business partner had to say, it appears we've got a pretty good idea of who the killer is." But even as he uttered the words, serious doubts were forming in his mind.

The chief walked slowly to the other side of the room, taking in the details. "Only the desk is disturbed," he said aloud. "We'll have no way of knowing whether the killer took something, until we talk to the family."

Holmlund nodded. "We found two letters on the floor by the desk from someone in Cleveland, Ohio, but the name wasn't Warren. The killer didn't take them, so evidently it wasn't what he was after."

"Anything else?"

"We found another golf club that was partially under the desk. Might have gotten knocked over during the attack. And that picture of Mrs. Paine."

"Did you look over the rest of the house?" Cusack asked.

The detectives had done a cursory inspection. They were looking for a potential murder weapon and were particularly interested in the cocktail bottle Ed had brought home the night before. It was larger than the one found in the room with the cheese and crackers, and the detectives thought it possible that the container could have been used as a murder weapon. The bottle, however, could not be found, and no other potential weapon had surfaced.

"I thought you said Burdick didn't drink liquor."

Holmlund shrugged. "The cook says he doesn't."

The chief's brow furrowed. Deceit and misdirection seemed to hang over the crime scene like a heavy fog. Clues were everywhere, cleverly arranged and contradictory. Viewing the crime scene gave him the same sensation as witnessing a skillful conjuring trick.

"We are quite sure there is nothing at all missing from the house?" Cusack asked aloud.

"It seems so, according to Katie. We want confirmation from the family," Holmlund replied. "Dr. Marcy asked us not to disturb them any more today."

Cusack snorted. It was not the place of a physician to dictate how the police would investigate. "We shall have to disturb them now," he told the detectives. He looked at his pocket watch. It was nearly 2:00 p.m. "I'll take Mrs. Hull, and you fellows can question the children."

The police entered the kitchen and found Maggie Murray removing her coat. "Been out, Maggie?" Cusack asked casually.

"Yes, sir," Maggie replied. "Mrs. Hull sent me on an errand."

Not wanting to appear overly interested, Cusack merely commented that it was very cold to be out running errands unless Maggie had gone somewhere close by.

Maggie removed her hat. "Only back to the drugstore. She wanted a telegram sent to Mrs. Burdick in Atlantic City."

"What was the message?" Cusack demanded.

"T'isn't long," Maggie said. "Here's what she gave me."

Cusack took the slip of paper from the cook's outstretched hand. The words, written in tall, spidery script, read:

Come home. Mr. Burdick is dead.

Without asking, Cusack stuffed the paper into his pocket. "Maggie, please ask Mrs. Hull and the children to come downstairs. We need to ask them a few questions before we leave. We'll be brief."

"I'm afraid that's impossible," said a male voice behind them. Cusack wheeled to find Dr. Marcy and Charles Parke standing behind him. Surprised to find the two men were still in the house, the chief did not immediately answer.

The doctor's face was flushed. "As I mentioned to your detectives here earlier, I am the family physician, and I object to you questioning them. Mrs. Hull and the children have suffered a severe shock."

"I understand, doctor," Cusack answered mildly. "But it is not at all our intent to distress the family. I fear we are obliged to question them today."

"It's out of the question, sir," Dr. Marcy said, with unusual energy. "I cannot, will not allow their health to be put at risk. I've treated Mrs. Hull for four years for her heart." He glanced at Charles Parke.

Burdick's business partner cleared his throat. "As Ed's friend and the guardian of the children, I must agree with Dr. Marcy. I will strenuously advise them to ensure their attorney is present if they do eventually need to be questioned."

"Their attorney?" Cusack echoed in disbelief. "The family are not under suspicion, sir."

"It's merely a precaution," Parke said.

For a moment, Cusack was undecided but he gave in with little grace. If they pursued the interviews with Mrs. Hull and the children at the moment, they would hold up other important aspects of the investigation. He found Dr. Marcy's behavior to be highly suspicious and silently vowed to keep an eye on him. "We'll return tomorrow," he told the doctor firmly.

Just before the police left the Burdick home, Alice wired a response to her mother's telegram. She would leave Atlantic City on the 3:00 p.m. train and arrive in Buffalo by morning.

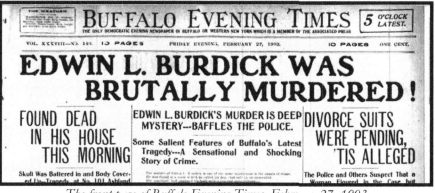

The front page of Buffalo Evening Times, February 27, 1903

The press had gotten the story early, and it quickly captivated the city of Buffalo, where the Burdicks were well-known. The story spread to other cities in New York, then to the surrounding states. Within two days, the brutal murder of the wealthy Edwin Burdick in his den was national news.

The Jigsaw Puzzle

Early in the evening, Chief Cusack returned to police headquarters. He learned, with mild surprise, that Alice had wired the police a duplicate of the message she sent to her mother. It had been sent from the Hotel Traymore, a ritzy resort in Atlantic City.

Atlantic City's Hotel Traymore, where Alice Burdick lived in January and February of 1903

Cusack checked the train table and determined she would arrive in Buffalo at 8:30 a.m. the following morning. He fully intended to speak to Mrs. Burdick, Mrs. Hull, and the children the following day.

His thoughts lingered on Dr. Marcy. The doctor deliberately interfered with the investigation at a dozen different points during the day. His claims of concern for his patients' health weren't particularly convincing, in the chief's opinion. *What interest does he have in this?* Cusack wondered.

Putting the telegram and his thoughts of Dr. Marcy aside, Chief Cusack opened his notebook to review its contents. He liked to treat his cases like jigsaw puzzles. Every event and all the oddities fit together, then the whole picture reveals itself. "Once I get the frame right, the pieces fall into place," was how he liked to explain it.

Cusack focused first on what he had learned about the victim. Ed Burdick was an unlikely candidate to be the victim of a violent homicide. He was a successful and respected man with a settled, structured life. He had three young children for whom he cared a great deal. From all the chief had gathered, Burdick was also a kind man with no known enemies—save Arthur Pennell.

His wife's affair with Pennell was unfortunate, but no one could say Burdick had been unreasonable or unforgiving. Only one man in a thousand would have taken his wife back three times in two years and still be generous enough to offer to share custody of the children with her and another man, Cusack thought.

Ed did not threaten the former friend who had broken up his marriage. He was neither violent nor consumed with bitterness. Instead, he tended to his business and his children. His personality and physique were small and meek; he was not at all the type of man whom one associated with intrigue of any kind.

It was clear that Ed Burdick's murderer was no stranger, so Chief Cusack focused on the victim's personal circumstances, looking for anything that might have produced the hatred required to kill him in such a fashion.

Arthur Pennell, of course, was the most obvious suspect: He threatened to kill the victim on more than one occasion, after all. He had a pressing motive. Had Ed Burdick lived a week longer, he would have divorced his wife, an action Pennell was apparently desperate to stop.

Cusack pondered this. Why was Pennell desperate to stop the divorce? According to Parke, Mrs. Burdick's paramour worried about some sort of inevitable disclosure. But if his wife was already aware of the affair, what disclosure did he fear? A loss of status, perhaps? Could he have been afraid that he would have to be financially responsible for Mrs. Burdick?

These musings brought to mind the letters the detectives found in Burdick's wallet. Parke said he didn't know where Ed got them, and the chief assumed Mrs. Burdick had hidden them in the house, and her husband had either searched for them or come across them by accident.

He pulled out the letters and read through them quickly. After he was finished, he read them again, more slowly. They contained no threats against

Burdick other than the one Holmlund had brought to his attention earlier, but they were woven through with a deep, wistful sadness.

Cusack was disturbed. Based on what he knew of the circumstances that led to the Burdicks' divorce, he had assumed Pennell was a rogue, the kind of man who would ruin another man's wife for the fun of it and feel no remorse. But the letters were not those of a man toying with a woman's heart. They were unmistakably the letters of a man who was frustrated in love.

The chief planned to question Pennell later that evening, but he wanted to learn everything he could before confronting him. In particular, he wanted to know if Pennell had an appointment with Burdick last night, or if he had been seen anywhere near Ashland Avenue.

If Arthur Pennell killed Ed Burdick, it would wrap up the case simply and easily. But Cusack's intuition told him this case was not so simple nor would it be solved easily. If Pennell committed the murder, some things simply didn't make sense. Why wasn't Burdick dressed? Who did the long hair belong to? Who was eating the food and drinking cocktails in his den? As unlikely as it appeared, the circumstances begged the question of whether Arthur Pennell was really the only person who might have wanted Burdick dead.

By midafternoon, the police learned about the countersuit Alice filed against Ed alleging he had been unfaithful to her with three women. Cusack had never met Alice, and indeed had only just become aware of her existence earlier in the day, but he already questioned her credibility. He seriously doubted the Burdick's marriage failed due to Ed's faithlessness.

However, if he gave Alice's accusations any credence, it opened a whole new field of speculation.

Helen Warren was the only woman actually named in Alice's countersuit. Police instantly recognized her name from the newspaper clipping about her divorce that was in Burdick's wallet. If Burdick had a love interest now, what of it? He and his wife were separated and would have been divorced by this time next week. Mrs. Warren was obviously divorced as well.

Nevertheless, the chief had to admit that it *did* matter if Ed had been pursuing another woman, especially if that woman happened to be the newly divorced Mrs. Warren.

When Alice made the complaint, Helen Warren was still married. If the accusation was true, Ed may have played a pivotal role in the Warrens' divorce.

If Burdick had broken up the Warrens' home, it was quite possible Mr. Warren would harbor hostile, even murderous sentiments toward him.

Helen Warren

At the very least, it was questionable that Burdick would carry a newspaper notice about the Warrens' divorce in his wallet.

The veiled reference to a socialite in Alice's complaint was widely interpreted to refer to Gertrude Paine. If Burdick had an affair with her, or wished to have an affair, Mrs. Paine's husband would presumably resent it. It was unusual—and a little unseemly—for a married man to have a photograph of a woman who was not his wife. It was difficult to ignore the symbolism of her picture being found on the den floor, a few feet away from Ed's battered body. Could the murderer have left it there as a grim calling card?

Mrs. Warren and Mrs. Paine were only two possibilities. There might be other angry husbands, or perhaps a woman who thought Burdick had played fast and loose with her affections. Cusack had difficulty picturing Ed Burdick as a modern-day Lothario, leaving a trail of broken hearts in his path. But anything was possible.

Reports of several anonymous suspects trickled in throughout the afternoon. The most credible report came from Patrolman August Meyers, whose beat was near the Burdick home. About midnight, he spotted a lone woman, nicely dressed, hurrying away from Ashland Avenue. Meyers said when she saw him, she dodged into the shadows and quickened her pace. At the time, he assumed she didn't realize he was a policeman and wanted to avoid meeting a stranger. But now he was suspicious. Two cab drivers reported dropping fares off in the vicinity of Ashland Avenue, whom the police later considered suspicious.

Cusack would investigate any lead thoroughly, but his gut instinct was the murderer was no mysterious stranger, but someone known to be close to Burdick. His mind wandered back to the open desk drawer and the scattered papers. It was possible the killer's object had not been murder. Perhaps he had come there only to take something then encountered Burdick and matters escalated. Cusack struggled with the idea, then shook his head.

In the chief's opinion, the biggest clue at the crime scene was the undeniable fact the killer remained in the house after the murder, taking pains to create the illusion that the murder was committed by a stranger during a botched robbery. This reinforced Cusack's belief that the murderer was no stranger. An actual stranger would have left as soon as possible and would have no reason to stage the scene.

The staging also strongly indicated Burdick's murderer had almost certainly been in the home before and knew it well. Who else would take the risk of going to another room to stage a crime scene after the murder? The killer apparently knew the other occupants of the house were asleep upstairs and that the kitchen had a window large enough for a person to crawl through.

His thoughts moved forward. They knew for a fact that the murderer had not broken into the house. That left three possibilities.

The first possibility was that the murderer had a key to the house and let himself in. If that were the case, it put the focus squarely on Pennell, who could have easily used Alice's key or had a duplicate made. According to Maggie, when she came in at 10:18 p.m. through the back door, Burdick heard her come in and came out to investigate. The chief remembered the loaded revolver in the den. Ed Burdick was a man on edge.

The front door was much closer to the den than the back door. If the murderer used a key, presumably Burdick would have heard him too. Cusack could not envision a scenario in which Burdick would hear someone enter the house and not go out to investigate. He would have gone out to the hallway and confronted the intruder there. Talking or shouting would have awakened at least some of the household. And, very likely, the murder would have happened outside the den. Yet the murder obviously had taken place in the den, and Burdick knew the person was there.

The murderer could have entered the house with a key several hours earlier, but he would have had to conceal himself somewhere in the house. The medical examiner said Burdick died around 2:00 a.m., which meant the murderer would have waited for several hours to kill Burdick, even though he was alone downstairs reading. Cusack rejected this possibility as unrealistic.

The second possibility was that the murderer lived in the house. The children certainly could be ruled out, but Mrs. Hull, Maggie Murray, and Katie Koenig had to be considered. The police would be returning to the Burdick home, and all three women would be questioned. Mrs. Hull had a possible motive, if she was angry at Ed for ordering her daughter to leave. Even if that was the case, would Mrs. Hull have been capable of committing such a murder? According to Dr. Marcy, she was exceedingly frail. And would she really rob the children, to whom she was devoted, of their father? Maggie and Katie were more plausible, but nothing indicated they would have any desire to hurt their employer. Nevertheless, Cusack would see that they were questioned.

The third possibility was that Ed let the killer in to the house, which Cusack privately believed to be the case. In this scenario, Burdick expected someone to come to his home and waited in the den for their arrival. The family would have been awakened if the doorbell was rung. It was an unusually loud bell, and Mrs. Hull and Maggie Murray claimed to be light sleepers. If Ed allowed the murderer in, he either opened the door at an agreed-upon time or listened for a tap on the door or window. Given Burdick's state of paranoia, his willingness to admit this person in the middle of the night and turn his back to them indicated a great deal of trust. The murderer must have had a deep antipathy toward Burdick but concealed it so well that the victim never suspected he was in danger.

Cusack's mind drifted back to the question of whether the murderer was male or female.

The crime scene certainly suggested a woman committed the murder. The clothes worn by the victim could not have been removed after the fact. They would have been covered in blood, like his undershirt. But Ed's smoking jacket, trousers, underwear, and socks were found near the divan, untorn and unstained.[XII] The clump of long hair found on the body's torso also pointed to a female killer. The detectives noticed that the root of each strand was visible and theorized Burdick managed to tear it from his assailant's head. They were hopeful that matching the hair to its owner might prove to be the key to identifying the murderer. [XIII] The tray of refreshments also suggested a woman, but Cusack conceded it could be another prop in the tableau the murderer created after killing Burdick.

Nevertheless, Cusack could scarcely imagine a woman committing so violent a murder. Could such a female exist? Unbidden, a line from his school days replayed itself in the chief's memory.

Heav'n has no Rage, like Love to Hatred turn'd,
Nor Hell a Fury, like a Woman scorn'd.

His mouth twisted into a grim smile; yes, a woman could have done it.

Cusack had to consider Mrs. Warren and Mrs. Paine to be suspects, quite as viable as their husbands. The fact Mrs. Pennell evidently knew of her husband's philandering did not eliminate her as a suspect, either. Ironically, the only person who could be definitively ruled out was Alice Burdick, the victim's estranged wife. The police had verified Mrs. Burdick was more than 400 miles away, in an Atlantic City hotel room, when her husband was murdered.

Superintendent William Bull suddenly appeared in his doorway, interrupting his reverie. Cusack rose and greeted his superior officer. "I've been at the morgue while the autopsy was conducted," Bull told him.

"Was that Howland conducting it?" Cusack inquired.

"Yes, him and Dr. Danser. Results are about what you'd expect."

"Anything new, sir?"

Bull shrugged. "According to Howland, Burdick had an unusually thin skull. Said he'd been hit probably 15, 20 times. They took samples to the chemist to test for poison, but I don't expect that'll bring much to light. They said there were no signs of poison that they saw." [xiv]

A few minutes after Bull departed, Detectives Holmlund and Sullivan came in to provide their updates.

They had spent the afternoon tracking the known suspects to ascertain their whereabouts for the past 24 hours. They had learned some things about the Pennells, the Warrens, and the Paines.

"Start with Pennell," Cusack directed.

The detectives had interviewed two acquaintances of Arthur Pennell who said the attorney purchased a revolver three weeks earlier.

The detectives visited Wallbridge's, the hardware store where he purchased the gun. E.W. Fox, the clerk, remembered Pennell well, for he had returned that very morning, just hours after Ed's body was discovered, to purchase another gun. When the clerk expressed surprise at his buying another gun so soon, Pennell said the first gun had been stolen. [xii]

Burdick, of course, had not been shot. Still, the primary suspect purchasing two guns within a few weeks, including on the day of the murder, seemed like quite a coincidence.

Detective Sullivan had also found a man who regularly tended the Pennells' furnace. Henry Orrett arrived as usual that morning about 9:30 a.m., but to his surprise, Arthur had put the coal on already. "He said Pennell had never done that before," Sullivan explained. "He said Pennell didn't appear to be agitated in any way and greeted him like he always did."

The detectives learned that Dr. Paine had been away all week. He practiced dentistry in Batavia throughout the week and came home to be with his wife and child on the weekends. Mrs. Paine took in two boarders to help make ends meet.

Their other update concerned Mrs. Warren, of Cleveland, Ohio. The Cleveland Police Department verified that Helen Warren was at home on the night of the murder. [XIII] Her ex-husband, J. Burton Warren, was traveling for business and had not yet been located.

"We'll keep digging, chief, but it's unlikely Warren had anything to do with it, in my opinion," Detective Sullivan offered.

"Yes," Cusack agreed. "But we need to eliminate him as a suspect. You didn't speak directly to Mr. or Mrs. Warren, did you?"

"No, sir," Sullivan replied. The only person the detectives had managed to reach was Mrs. Warren's father, Julius Cleveland, who indignantly refuted the rumor that Ed Burdick had broken up his daughter's marriage.

"Mrs. Warren's maiden name is Cleveland," Cusack observed with a smile. "Thank goodness she married, eh? Might have got confusing with her living in Cleveland."

"It's a funny thing, that," Sullivan said thoughtfully. "It's not a coincidence. Evidently, she's a descendant of the man they named the city for."

"You don't say."

"One other thing, chief," Holmlund added. "Those letters that were postmarked from Cleveland were from Mrs. Warren's father. They didn't contain anything of significance—just business letters. Mr. Cleveland said he didn't send Burdick that newspaper clipping."

Chief Cusack would not be satisfied without officially ruling out Mr. Warren, but he had to admit it looked like a dead end.

The Police Are Denied

The longer the murderer had to cover his tracks, get rid of evidence, or invent an alibi, the harder it would be to solve the case. Therefore, Chief Cusack directed the detectives to lose no time interviewing the suspects and witnesses.

A group of five policeman approached 492 Elmwood Avenue, the residence of Dr. and Mrs. Paine, at nine o'clock that evening. After a whispered conference, they took positions around the perimeter of the house, one man at each corner. Lights shone from the upstairs windows, but the ground floor was dark.

Detective Holmlund knocked on the door three times. At last, a middle-aged man with thick glasses opened the door and peered at the policeman on the front porch curiously.

"Yes?" he asked, with a heavy accent that the detective recognized as Swedish. "I help you?"

Detective Holmlund introduced himself and said he needed to speak with Mrs. Paine.

"You want to speak Mrs. Paine tonight?" the man asked doubtfully.

"It's important, or I wouldn't bother her," Holmlund replied.

When the man still hesitated, Holmlund, whose parents had immigrated from Sweden, had an idea. He appealed to the man in broken Swedish, telling him he was a police officer and pointing to his badge. "Jag är polis."

Holmlund's hunch was correct. The man immediately brightened at the sound of his native language and became compliant. He eagerly introduced himself: "Jag heter Carlson."

"Good to meet you, Mr. Carlson," Holmlund said. "May I see Mrs. Paine now?"

Mr. Carlson stepped back. "Come in, please." He moved to a light fixture on the wall and turned the gaslight up to illuminate the room.

"Wait here," he said. "I call Mrs. Paine." Carlson hurried off, and Holmlund examined his surroundings. The parlor was a medium-sized room, not as large as the Burdick home, but the furnishings and décor were beautiful and ornate. A few dolls occupied one corner. Holmlund stooped to pick one up and gingerly placed it in a large wooden box that seemed to serve as a toy chest.

"Mr. Holmlund?"

The detective turned to see Carlson standing in the doorway, looking at him apologetically.

"Mrs. Paine is coming downstairs?" he asked.

Carlson shook his head. "She says no. She says her husband not here and for you to return when he is here." The man looked at the floor nervously. "I'm to send you away."

"All right, Mr. Carlson. We will come back soon," Holmlund said, to the intense relief of the man. "Dr. Paine is home this weekend?"

Carlson nodded eagerly and added, "I rent a room here."

Holmlund thanked him and left. He wasn't sure how to interpret Gertrude Paine's refusal to come downstairs. Was she defiant or perhaps frightened? In any event, she did not seem eager to help find the murderer of her friend Ed Burdick.

Half an hour after Holmlund departed, the telephone in the Paine home rang. Mrs. Paine answered it herself. It was a reporter from *The Buffalo Enquirer*. "Is this Mrs. Gertrude Paine?" he asked, after introducing himself.

She confirmed she was.

"Did officers visit your house this evening in connection with the Burdick murder?"

The Enquirer tended to print more salacious stories, but Gertrude seized the opportunity to vent and continued to talk with the reporter. "My husband was out of town, and I would not see the officers. He has been out of town since Monday. He practices in Batavia and only comes home once a week."

Gertrude said she had spoken to her husband via telephone and told them about the police coming by. "I told him to call the district attorney, but he said if the police wanted any information he had about the Burdicks, he would come to Buffalo. He'll be here tomorrow morning."

The reporter asked if Gertrude knew the Burdicks well.

"Yes, I knew Mr. Burdick, and I know Mrs. Burdick," she responded. With growing annoyance, she added, "I don't see why the police should come to us for information. We know them no better than lots of others living in the neighborhood."

"Weren't you a member of the Red Jacket Golf Club with Mr. and Mrs. Burdick?" the reporter persisted.

"No!" Gertrude cried. "I have nothing further to say, other than that I am sorry my husband's and my own name were dragged into this case by the police. As I said, my husband has not been in Buffalo since Monday." Fuming, she replaced the receiver. But Gertrude Paine certainly had not heard the last of the press.

A Visit to Arthur Pennell

When the detectives reconvened at police headquarters, Cusack was talking with a small, wiry man with a receding hairline. They recognized the chief's companion as Erie County's District Attorney Edward Coatsworth. When the murderer was identified and put on trial, DA Coatsworth would prosecute the case, and he wanted to be present when the detectives questioned Pennell.

A little after 11:00 p.m., Cusack, Coatsworth, Sullivan, and Holmlund stood on the doorstep of 208 Cleveland Avenue. A maid opened the door to the narrow, three-story home. She blinked in surprise and confusion at seeing four men on the porch so late. Cusack asked if they could see Mr. Pennell, and the maid asked them to wait while she asked if Mr. and Mrs. Pennell were at home for visitors. A moment later, she opened the door wide and asked them to come in.

208 Cleveland Avenue, the home of Arthur and Carrie Pennell

The Pennells were still up and sitting in their parlor. Arthur rose to greet them. He had known they would be coming, but he was no less nervous than if their visit had surprised him.

Carrie Pennell greeted the men civilly but excused herself at once. She did not want to be in the room to hear the inevitable questions about Alice Burdick or listen to her husband's replies. The police allowed her to go but informed her they wanted to speak with her before they left.

Mrs. Pennell assented and retired to her bedroom to write to her sister. Her letter gives us a little insight into the way she saw the connection between her family and the Burdicks.

"I feel sometimes as if I could not stand up under the strain, yet for Arthur's sake I must," Carrie Pennell wrote. "It is harder for him than for me, as he is so sensitive and has such pride and honor. To think that all this trouble should come to us through our efforts to aid others."

Downstairs, Arthur Pennell sat down with the police and asked how he could help them.

Chief Cusack had informed the others he would take the lead asking the questions. He began in a brisk, formal voice. "Mr. Pennell, you've heard by now that Ed Burdick was murdered early this morning."

"Yes, sir," Arthur replied gravely. His face was impassive.

Cusack attempted subtlety. "In the course of our investigation, we've learned about the Burdicks' divorce. We understand that you have been intimately involved in the details."

Arthur's face flushed, and after a moment he said, "Yes, I am Mrs. Burdick's legal representation."

"And a close friend to Mr. and Mrs. Burdick at one time, we understand?"

"Yes." After a momentary silence, Arthur added, "Gentlemen, I am not prepared to answer any personal questions about Mr. or Mrs. Burdick this evening. I've only just learned of the tragedy, and I fear I wouldn't be able to answer you with much clarity. I am, however, happy to oblige if you have questions about myself."

Cusack had anticipated this, and he did not intend to compel Pennell to talk about his relationship with Alice Burdick, at least not at the moment. His real objective was to search the premises.

"Mr. Pennell, we're asking everyone close to Burdick to give a detailed account of their movements from yesterday afternoon until this morning. We also ask for your permission to search your home."

Arthur listened attentively and nodded. "You may search the house, if you like. You'll find nothing of an incriminating nature here." Chief Cusack grunted noncommittally.

"As to my movements yesterday," Pennell continued. "I can tell you in detail. I rose at my usual time and went to work after breakfast. At 10 a.m., I stepped out to run some errands and afterwards had my usual shave."

"Where was that?" Coatsworth interrupted.

"At the Iroquois barbershop. After luncheon, I continued to work through the afternoon. I came directly home after work, as I usually do. Mrs. Pennell and I sat down to dinner together—oh, around 7:20 or 7:30."

Cusack looked up briefly and saw Detective Holmlund had pulled a small notebook from his pocket and began scribbling notes. Cusack turned back to Arthur Pennell. "Go on."

"After dinner, I went to the automobile station on West Utica Street. My automobile needed some minor repairs." In response to Cusack's follow-up questions, the attorney estimated he arrived at approximately 8:30 p.m. He chatted with Mr. Babcock, the mechanic who was making the repairs, for several minutes.

The Pennell home was less than a mile from where the Burdicks lived. Walking from one house to the other would take about 15 minutes. West Utica Street is between the two houses, and a mere 5-minute walk to Ashland Avenue.

"Yes, sir. What did you do next?"

Pennell said he had come directly home afterward without making additional stops. "I expect I was out for perhaps an hour after dinner. When I returned to my home, my wife and I sat together for some time. I was reading, and I believe she was writing letters."

"What did you do then?"

Pennell said he had not left his house again that evening. "I retired around 10:00 p.m., and my wife came to bed shortly afterward."

"At what hour did you awaken?"

"Around 7:00 a.m. I'm not certain as to the exact time."

"When did you learn of the murder?"

"Around noon. My secretary learned of it somehow and informed me. Later, I purchased the evening papers."

"Do you have any weapons in the house, Mr. Pennell?" Coatsworth asked suddenly.

"Why, yes," Pennell replied in a surprised tone. "I purchased a revolver just this morning, at the hardware store."

"Why did you buy a gun today, sir?"

"I'd actually purchased a gun three weeks ago, but it was stolen. This gun replaced the first."

"Were you anywhere near the Burdick home yesterday or today?"

"No, sir."

Cusack stole a glance at Coatsworth. The DA's disappointment was obvious. Arthur Pennell was a likeable person, and he seemed to be answering their questions in a truthful, straightforward manner. They would verify all of it, of course, but Pennell gave at least the appearance of a man answering questions honestly.

A drawing of Arthur Pennell, circa 1903

According to an article that ran the following day in a local newspaper, "Arthur R. Pennell is a good-looking man, less than 40 years old. He is known in Buffalo society and has a good reputation as a lawyer. His eyes will attract the attention of a person because of their remarkable alertness and observing power. He has a mustache trained somewhat in the Emperor William style. Pennell is a man of ordinary physique and carries his 160 pounds with grace. He has a neat little home at No. 208 Cleveland Avenue, and among friends seemed to be all that a loving husband could be to a wife. Mrs. Pennell is well-liked among her associates." [xv]

Cusack asked to speak with Mrs. Pennell, and Arthur went to the door and called softly, "Lizzie! Please tell Mrs. Pennell our visitors wish to see her."

He turned back to his visitors. "I'll excuse myself, gentlemen. If you should want anything more from me, I'll be nearby."

"Thank you, Mr. Pennell," Cusack said. "If you don't mind, we'll send two of our detectives with you now to begin the search, and we shall assist after we speak with Mrs. Pennell. As soon as the search is complete, we can be on our way."

"Of course," Arthur said quietly. He left, closing the door noiselessly behind him. Cusack looked after him, trying to pinpoint the emotion with which Pennell seemed to be wrestling. It certainly wasn't guilt, nor was it anger. It wasn't sadness, exactly. The answer came to him at once, as clearly as though someone had spoken the word aloud: *Shame.*

A few moments later, Carrie Pennell swept into the room and gracefully seated herself. The dignified Mrs. Pennell looked older than her 38 years. As a leading member of the Buffalo chapter of the Daughters of the American Revolution and numerous organizations and charities, she frequently spoke at luncheons and benefit receptions. Over time, she had developed poise. In this case, her self-possession was more remarkable because it contrasted so vividly with her husband's uneasiness.

Chief Cusack's questioning of Mrs. Pennell was brief. He asked about her husband's activities over the past 24 hours. Carrie corroborated all the key points Arthur had told them. Mrs. Pennell appeared to be sincere but the police weren't especially impressed with a wife corroborating her husband's alibi.

Cusack asked about relations between Ed Burdick and her husband. Mrs. Pennell's face betrayed no emotion. "I believe they quarreled," she replied composedly. "Though I'm not certain."

"Thank you, Mrs. Pennell," Chief Cusack said. He got to his feet, signaling the interview was as at end. "We'll join the others now, and be on our way as quickly as possible."

Mrs. Pennell

The police searched every inch of the Pennell home and grounds, from the furnace grate to the cobwebbed attic. They were looking for anything incriminating but were especially keen to find bloody clothing. The crime scene was excessively bloody and the killer must have gotten blood on himself—or herself. They found nothing at all to tie either of the Pennells to the crime. At last, Cusack thanked the couple for their graciousness, and the visitors took their leave.

Even with all four men working as quickly as possible, the search had taken almost 90 minutes. It was nearly 1:00 a.m. The police emerged from Pennell home and into the freezing winter air. They bid one another farewell and headed for home. Cusack did not notice the biting cold, nor the sound of his boots on the packed snow as he trudged homeward. He was thinking about Arthur Pennell and the same unpleasant sensation he had felt in Burdick's den crept over him again. Things were not what they appeared to be, and the obvious answer was not the right answer.

The chief could not rule out Arthur Pennell as Ed Burdick's murderer, but his instinct told him to look elsewhere for the responsible party.

Alice Comes Home

A little before 8:30 a.m. Saturday morning, a train arrived in Buffalo. Alice Burdick alighted on the platform, wearing a smart, tailored gray suit and carrying a leather pocketbook. She looked around expectantly, as though searching for a particular face in the crowd. Not finding it, she put her head down and walked briskly, as though wishing to avoid recognition. It was far too late for that.

Two reporters were there, with a photographer, and only the presence of a policeman prevented the latter from photographing Alice. A reporter from *The Buffalo Enquirer* approached her first. "I know nothing of the details," Alice said, in answer to his questions. "Only what I could guess from the telegram my mother sent to me."

The reporter said Mr. Burdick had been bludgeoned to death in his den and wanted to know if Mrs. Burdick knew of anyone in Buffalo who wanted to hurt her husband.

Alice had only been notified that Ed was dead, but she accepted the news that he had been violently murdered without any visible agitation. "God forbid that I know any such person," she replied. When the reporter pressed her, she added, "I don't suspect a soul on earth. I never heard Ed say he was afraid of anyone or that his life had been threatened."

"You know that last night, the district attorney and several detectives searched Mr. and Mrs. Pennell's home?" a second reporter asked. "What have you to say about Mr. and Mrs. Pennell?"

"Arthur Pennell and Ed Burdick always got along together," Alice declared emphatically. "They had no quarrels. *I say no quarrels.* I never heard of one." She turned back to the first reporter and asked: "It was in the den, you say? Ed so liked that room. That little gathering of pillows and lounging places captured his heart. His pride and joy seemed to be the appearance of that room. To think that that was the place he was murdered."

The reporters asked about Mrs. Paine and Mrs. Warren, but Alice didn't answer these questions. The more persistent of the two reporters tried another question. "Can you give any clue that might lead to the discovery of your husband's murderer?"

"My mind is collected," she said, with a bright smile. "But if my life were at stake, I couldn't tell you anything about the murderer. It will be the aim of my life to run to earth Ed Burdick's slayer. God will help me. While there may have been at times some very slight difficulties between Ed and myself, still our love was mutual."

"Do you believe your husband was a ladies' man and had connections outside the home that would lead to the divorce court?"

"My husband," Alice replied. "Was a stunning and clever dresser and was naturally attractive to women. As to his outside life, I cannot state facts."

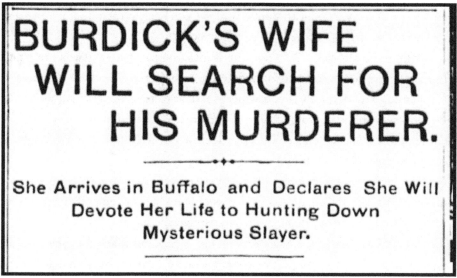

BURDICK'S WIFE WILL SEARCH FOR HIS MURDERER.

She Arrives in Buffalo and Declares She Will Devote Her Life to Hunting Down Mysterious Slayer.

Alice vowed to find Ed's killer.

She nodded as the police officer beckoned to her. The widow's cab had arrived. "You will have to excuse me," she said. "My mother is waiting for me. But I will aid the authorities in sending the murderer, if ever he or she is caught, to the electric chair." XVI

The officer helped her thread her way through the crowd and opened the cab door for her. When Alice emerged from the carriage in front of 101 Ashland Avenue, her mother and three children greeted her affectionately.

She had no plans to return to Atlantic City or to leave her beautiful home in Buffalo again.

A small knot of reporters stood in front of the Austin building, where Arthur Pennell's primary office was located. It was Saturday, but he could not rest and had gone to his office. When he stepped outside, they rushed up to him. "This horrible case," Arthur muttered under his breath. Then in his normal speaking voice, he said, "I am sorry, heartily sorry, and pained over this terrible affair. I am unable to explain anything. Not that I would withhold anything that would aid in solving the mystery, but I cannot. I am unable to tell anything. I'm unable to do so."

He confirmed he had been named as corespondent in Ed Burdick's divorce suit against Alice.

"Have you quarreled with Burdick or have you been as friendly as it is possible for men to be friendly under such circumstances?"

Arthur shrank back. "I do not care to discuss that matter. It will not help." But just as quickly, he changed his mind. "We have been as friendly as it is possible for men to be under such circumstances ... The facts of the case are these: Mr. Burdick sued his wife for a divorce, and in his complaint, he made me the corespondent. She defended the case, denied the allegations, and brought in countercharges. That is all."

The reporter asked about Mrs. Burdick's whereabouts. "In the city—I presume she is in the city. She was expected here." He vehemently denied Alice was in Buffalo Thursday night and reiterated that she had been in Atlantic City.

"There has been some talk that you and Mrs. Pennell are going to obtain a separation. District Attorney Coatsworth has said he had information that you and Mrs. Burdick were going to divorce your spouses."

Arthur's face flushed a deep red. "I do not care to say anything on that point." He excused himself.

The newspaper reporter's assessment of the conversation was that "[Pennell] appeared extremely nervous and the murder and subsequent disclosures have completely unnerved him." XVII

Window into the Whirlwind

In the days following the murder, details of the Burdicks' unhappy marriage and impending divorce seeped out in the newspapers. As the investigation progressed, the papers printed the speculation that the murderer could be a woman connected to Burdick's domestic trouble.

The people of Buffalo were shocked by what they read. They had always suspected something sinister about the Elmwood Avenue set. Now they could see the stories and rumors about them were far from smoke and mirrors or invented intrigue. Rather, they were like a smoking volcano, and the murder was the inevitable eruption.

Photographs of Ed and Alice Burdick

The scandalous nature of the case caused newspapers as far away as San Francisco to print regular updates about the case. Besides implicating "prominent, fashionable families," the case was interesting because of Edwin himself. "Mr. Burdick is shown to have been a mild-mannered Don Juan. The police have evidence of dozens of affairs in which he is said to have figured, and prominent names are connected with the case." [XVIII]

To the delight of Buffalo readers, Dr. Seth Paine, husband of the glamorous Gertrude Paine, consented to be interviewed about Ed Burdick's murder, following a talk he had with the police. Dr. Paine practiced dentistry in Batavia, a city located approximately 40 miles northeast of Buffalo. Dr. Paine spent the majority of each week in Batavia, and he was there on the night of the murder. The newspapers described the dentist as a stocky man with graying dark hair.

The dentist expressed his shock that anyone wanted to hurt Ed. Though he could not imagine who could be responsible for killing Burdick, he scoffed at the idea of a female murderer. "I don't believe that Eddie Burdick was killed by a woman. It was a man who was murderously angry at him. For what reason the crime was committed, I cannot think." [XIX]

"What about Arthur Pennell?" the reporter asked skeptically.

Dr. Paine shook his head at the mention of Pennell's name, but conceded the murderer must have known the house well. "I am sorry to hear of these divorce proceedings and the newspaper talk regarding Pennell. Pennell, as you know, was a member of the Elmwood Dancing Club, and, of course, was a friend of Mr. and Mrs. Burdick. I do not and cannot believe that Pennell was very friendly with Mrs. Burdick."

The paper eagerly questioned Dr. Paine about Ed Burdick. The dentist struggled to find the right words to describe his friend. Finally, he said, "Burdick was this kind of chap: Suppose your wife, and Smith's wife, and Burdick's wife were attending a social affair. Burdick would not show distinction in his gift of flowers or such. He would go to a flower store and buy bunches of violets for every one of the women in his crowd." [XX]

Despite his pronouncement that "Eddie Burdick was all that would make a ladies' man," Dr. Paine appeared unconcerned about his wife's relationship with his friend. He merely said he and Gertrude got along well with Ed and Alice. When Burdick encountered Mrs. Paine downtown, he bought her soda or candy and often walked a block or two with her.

Seth Paine said as far as he knew his wife had not seen Burdick in weeks but admitted he was not certain. "I never keep tabs on Mrs. Paine," he declared emphatically. "If she wanted to go out at 1:00 a.m., I would not ask her where she was going."

A reporter asked about the photograph of Mrs. Paine found in Burdick's den. The dentist shook his head. "I can't understand it, but I believe Burdick stole that photograph. There was nothing intimate between my wife and Eddie Burdick, and you can put that down in your newspapers in red ink." xx

Dr. Seth Paine

Some people, particularly those who were friendly with the victim, objected to the salacious reports about Ed Burdick in the newspapers. "They deny absolutely that he is an immoral man," *The Buffalo Times* reported. "They say he loved his home and his devotion to his children was not exceeded by that displayed by any other father in Buffalo. In fact, they claim his whole life was bound up in his children and that he would not defile that home by inviting a woman there for other than the most strictly honorable reason." XXI

One man, who would not give his name but claimed to be a "close and intimate friend of the family," said the Warrens, the Pennells, and the Burdicks used to be good friends. "Mrs. Warren was well-cultivated and educated. She was beautiful and charming. Burdick liked her very much... When she and her husband moved to Cleveland some three years ago, Burdick went down on several occasions to see her, he told me. He said he liked her company. I do not think there was anything wrong in those visits, as he admired her greatly."

When asked if Burdick was keen to get a divorce so he could marry Mrs. Warren, the friend replied, "I'm told it was Mr. Burdick's intention to marry Mrs. Warren when he was free. Mrs. Burdick didn't like this. She had a detective agency shadow her husband for months to obtain evidence against him. I was told she secured nothing because Burdick was a discreet man." The friend cautioned, "I only know one side of the story, that told to me by Burdick." XXII

And even those who did not know the victim personally had trouble reconciling themselves to the idea of the formal Mr. Burdick entertaining anonymous women downstairs while his three daughters and his estranged wife's mother slept upstairs.

On Saturday, February 28, Reverend Levi Powers, the minister at Church of the Messiah, hurried up the front steps of 101 Ashland Avenue and rang the doorbell. He glanced at his pocket watch and relaxed when he saw the time was 4:30. He was on time.

Katie opened the door and ushered him in. Powers was expected.

The minister greeted Katie somberly and inquired about the family in hushed tones. "Mrs. Burdick is waiting to speak to you upstairs," she replied, as she relieved the minister of his hat and coat. "I'll show you up."

The undertaker brought Ed's body home an hour ago, but Alice had not been downstairs. She was upstairs in the bedroom she had shared with her husband for many years. Since he had ordered her to leave three months earlier, Ed had slept there alone. His books covered the nightstand, and his clothes hung in the closet. Yet, improbably, it would be her bedroom again.

When Reverend Powers appeared, he offered Alice his condolences in a formal manner. Mrs. Burdick was nearly a stranger to him, despite having been a member of his congregation for many years. He knew Mrs. Hull fairly well. He spoke to her on Sundays and she had alluded to the domestic troubles in the Burdick home. Powers had also counseled Ed about his marital difficulties, and urged him to reconcile with his wife.

He asked Alice if she would like him to pray with her, and she consented quietly. A few moments later, the minister rose and told her he would wait downstairs with Mrs. Hull.

"Take as much time as you need," he told her. "When you are ready, we will begin."

Rev. Levi Powers

Reverend Powers returned to the ground floor and found his way to the front parlor. In 1903, most funerals were conducted at the home of the deceased. The furniture had been moved out to make way for Ed's closed casket, which was placed at far end of the room. A few chairs, evidently intended for the mourners, were clustered near the doorway where he stood, facing away from the casket.

Powers spotted Katie hurrying down the hall and waylaid her. "What time are the guests arriving?" he demanded. "It's ten minutes to five."

Katie shook her head. "Besides the family, there's just Mr. Parke and Mr. Stowell," she replied. "They're in the dining room having tea."

Reverend Powers frowned but said nothing. He knew Ed had many friends and acquaintances and he was saddened so few people were present to mourn this kind and generous man. For a moment, he wondered if the speed with which the arrangements were made was due to a lack of feeling on the part of Ed's estranged wife. His brow cleared as he recalled the telephone conversation he'd had the day before with Mrs. Hull. She had requested that he officiate a brief service the following afternoon, and mentioned Ed's body would be taken to his hometown of Canastota Sunday, where his mother and sister still lived. Reverend Powers concluded there would be a larger service there for family and friends to attend.

Unbeknownst to Powers, Ed's mother and sister had received a telegram from Mrs. Hull only six hours earlier, informing them of Ed's death and noting the funeral would take place in Buffalo within a few hours. The town of Canastota was situated 175 miles east of Buffalo. Delivering this horrible news only hours before the funeral effectively precluded Ed's family from being present for the service. However, Mrs. Hull's telegram stated that the family would bring the body to Canastota for interment in the morning.

The local friends, associates, and neighbors who lived close by and would have wanted to be present were not there either. Throughout the morning and early afternoon, horrified friends had come to the house, anxious to learn more of Ed's terrible fate and to offer help and condolences to the family. One by one, Katie met them at the door and turned them away, saying Mrs. Burdick was unable to see anyone. She took care not to mention the funeral; only Mr. Parke and Mr. Stowell were invited.

Reverend Powers pulled some notes he had written for the service from his pocket and reviewed them until Alice entered the room. She had changed into a dark blue dress with an intricate collar. She glanced at the casket but did not go near it. She chose the chair closest to the door and sat down. Her daughters filed in silently behind her and took their seats.

Charles Parke escorted Mrs. Hull in, and Mr. Stowell hurried in last. When everyone was seated, Reverend Powers began to speak.

"Man is born into trouble as the sparks fly upward. It is the Lord's mercy that we are not consumed by the flames because his compassion faileth not. The Lord will not cast us off forever."

The minister paused and his eye fell upon the solemn faces of the Burdick daughters. He felt especially sorry for them. "He causes grief, yet he will have compassion. There is nothing which shall not be manifested. Therefore, judge nothing, until the time the Lord brings to light the hidden things of darkness and makes manifest the councils of the heart.

"The solution lies beyond the upmost reach of our capacities. We will not abandon the old trust that there is a solution, without which this life of sorrow, pain, and misery becomes meaningless and impossible."

Reverend Powers paused impressively before delivering his closing thought. "There is room enough and time enough in the vast worlds and long years for God to fulfill himself to our understanding and satisfy our hearts. Amen."

The next morning, the family rose early and prepared to accompany Ed's body to Canastota, where he would be buried. As they were eating breakfast, a message arrived from Chief Cusack. Alice skimmed it and, with a sigh, passed it to Mrs. Hull. It was a courtesy notice that the police would be conducting a thorough search of the home while the family was away for the day.

When they reached Canastota, the family went directly to the cemetery. Ed would be buried in his family plot beside his father and his recently-deceased older sister, Genevieve Stowell.

A small crowd awaited the family at the gravesite. Ed's mother, Harriet Burdick, wept and leaned on the arm of her daughter, Lillian Willett, for support. The elder Mrs. Burdick was nearly paralyzed with grief. In just two months, she had lost two of her three children. She wanted to see her son, but friends of the family had read the newspaper accounts of Ed's violent death and feared what the sight of his mutilated body would do to his mother's failing health. They persuaded her not to have the casket opened.

A local minister conducted a short burial service.

A reporter from *The Buffalo Courier* followed the family east to Mr. Burdick's hometown, and was a witness to the sorrowful scene. He wrote in disbelief that the family spent less than an hour in the city. "The Eastern Express drew into the station at 1:30, 25 minutes late. By 2:19, the burial had been completed and Mrs. Burdick, her three daughters, and Mrs. Hull took the train for Buffalo.

"No tears had been shed and there was no evidence of emotion, except on the part of the murdered man's mother and sister," he added. "The minister offered prayers for 'the afflicted mother, sister, and other relatives.'" [xxiii] Alice Burdick was pointedly not mentioned.

Investigation and Rumors

The public interest in the Burdick murder took the police by surprise. Cusack had ordered continual surveillance of the Burdick, Pennell, and Paine homes by plainclothes officers. However, he soon modified his orders to ensure the officers were in uniform. The police were forced to continually disperse crowds of people. As the story grew, so did the number of reporters and morbid curiosity-seekers who stood gazing at the house, imagining the killer bolting from the front door and attempting to guess which windows belonged to the den.

The thorough search the police conducted of the Burdick property yielded no results. The family had left word for the police that they had identified one missing piece of property: Ed's heavy gold pocket watch had not been seen since his death. The detectives got a description of the watch from Katie. They suspected the murderer would pawn it as soon as possible to avoid the risk of keeping something so recognizable and incriminating.

Katie told the police one more interesting new detail: The Burdicks had a long-term houseguest. Mr. Hartzell, the family attorney, was staying in the home for the foreseeable future.

A photograph of the back of the Burdick home taken the weekend after the murder. The open kitchen window is marked with an X.

Coatsworth and Chief Cusack spoke to reporters as the weekend ended. Coatsworth was pessimistic. "There is nothing new. We haven't as many clues left as we had this morning. We are narrowing down the old clues."

Chief Cusack's update was more to the reporters' liking. "I'll state the crime looks as if it was committed by a woman. There isn't any doubt but what Burdick had an appointment in his den and that that appointment was with a woman. I am almost absolutely convinced that the crime was committed by a woman or that she was a witness or an accessory to the crime." XXIV

In truth, the police and the district attorney were more frustrated than they let on to the press. So far, each promising lead had fizzled, and the persons of interest whom the police and the DA thought could shed light onto the case were unable to be found, uncooperative, or had no information of value to offer.

Chief Cusack and Detective Holmlund interviewed Alice soon after she arrived Saturday morning. Though perfectly willing to talk, Alice could tell them nothing. When asked whether she knew of anyone who wanted to hurt her husband, Alice said that it must have been someone keen to stop the divorce proceedings, but she did not know who.

Coatsworth also spoke to Mrs. Hull again, attempting to get more information from her. He sensed she held many of the answers to the case, but she apparently had nothing to say about Ed Burdick, Arthur Pennell, nor her daughter that he did not already know.

The district attorney told Cusack privately that Mrs. Hull was evasive and deliberately unhelpful. Both were curious about the state of affairs between Alice Burdick and Arthur Pennell. Alice said she had sent Arthur a telegram before leaving Atlantic City to notify him of Ed's death and that she was coming home. Pennell, however, had been at Niagara Falls and was not at the train station to greet her. The officers who were surveilling the Burdick home knew Arthur Pennell had not visited her there and confirmed to the detectives that Alice had not left since returning to Buffalo, except to attend the burial in Canastota.

The police had worked night and day since the murder, attempting to learn as much as they could before the inquest into Ed's death, which was scheduled to begin March 14. The family, of course, would be prominent witnesses, as would the Pennells. The police were determined to identify the murderer and ascertain a clear picture of what happened to Ed Burdick by that time.

The beginning of the week brought several developments.

Early Monday morning, March 2, the medical examiner's office shared an important update with the police. After scrutinizing the hair found on the body's torso, they determined it was Ed's hair, torn violently from his scalp during the attack.

The detectives considered whether this news impacted their theory that Burdick was murdered by a woman, and they decided it did not. They thought the cushions piled upon the body pointed to a woman. The murderer had stayed in the room for some time, looking for something in the desk and staging the scene. A woman, they reasoned, would be unable to bear the site of Ed's horribly mutilated body so she put him out of sight that way. xxv

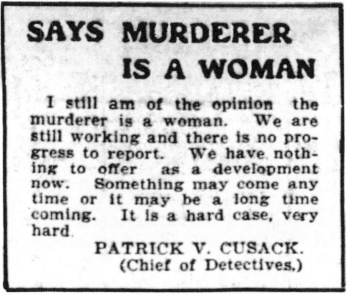

SAYS MURDERER IS A WOMAN

I still am of the opinion the murderer is a woman. We are still working and there is no progress to report. We have nothing to offer as a development now. Something may come any time or it may be a long time coming. It is a hard case, very hard.

PATRICK V. CUSACK.
(Chief of Detectives.)

The police were steadfast in their belief that a woman murdered Burdick.

At the time the Burdick murder was committed, the press was polite in their interactions with both the powerful and the powerless. They were less aggressive in pushing for details that were not germane to the topic. In most cases, they did not photograph a person without consent. Their relationship with the DA and the police was fairly good and mutually beneficial. The press got their story while the police and DA could use the press to cast a net for more information.

Though they were seen as a positive force overall, the press created many problems. The stories often were riddled with inaccuracies, ranging from misspellings to outright falsehoods. Final copy often included the home and business addresses of private citizens who were not accused of anything, and occasionally a photograph of their residence appeared in the newspapers. It was common practice to print rumors, unsubstantiated stories, and anonymous sourcing. False reports were rarely corrected.

In the Burdick case, the press significantly muddied the waters of the investigation. The most egregious example is the report of Ed's golf clubs in the den. Several newspapers falsely reported the maid had seen three golf clubs in the den on the Wednesday evening before Ed was murdered, but the putter was discovered to be missing in the chaos that followed. This was followed by incorrect reports that the police had since located the missing blood-stained putter but refused to say where they had located it. [XXVI] All of this was reported as fact, but later it was contradicted positively by the DA, who clarified that all three clubs were in the den when the body was discovered.

Other stories implicated residents based entirely upon speculation and hearsay. One story, published March 2, plainly referred to Gertrude Paine in asserting that "the finger of police suspicion in the Burdick murder mystery is pointing to a woman whose home is in the Elmwood district." [XXV]

Another story, citing unnamed sources, relayed an alleged incident at the Red Jacket Golf Club in which Ed Burdick was threatened by another club member who was not implicated in the case. According to the story, the man was upset that his wife had been seen with Ed multiple times. He shouted, "If I ever see you with my wife again, I'll kill you!" Ed's alleged response was that he would be ready for him and "let me say that if I find you repeating some of your performances, I'll kill you." [XXVII]

Besides the unfairness of implicating people this way, this type of reporting called into question the legitimacy of other, more important stories published in the same newspapers. Neither the public nor law enforcement uniformly accepted the newspapers as reliable sources of information.

For instance, *The Buffalo Courier* featured an interview on March 2 with a private detective whom Ed had hired to trail his wife and Pennell to gather information for his divorce suit. Detective John M. Boland told the *Courier* about the mountain of evidence he had gathered to support the Burdick divorce suit. "He said if Mrs. Burdick refused to leave his house, he would take measures to force her to go. He talked frequently about his mother-in-law, and said that at first she had seemed to stand with him in the family trouble, but later she had taken sides with her daughter." [XXVII]

If the information in the newspaper was accurate, it cast Burdick's domestic life in a new light and potentially changed the frame of the Chief Cusack's jigsaw puzzle. The police, however, dismissed the article as newspaper fodder.

District Attorney Coatsworth saw it differently. In his opinion, the new information had the potential to change the whole composition of the case. He still thought Arthur Pennell was most likely behind the murder, but as far as he was concerned, Mrs. Hull was a viable suspect.

At 11:30 a.m. Tuesday, March 3, Cusack entered the Buffalo Envelope Company. Ostensibly, he was there to search Ed's belongings for clues. His real objective was to meet with Charles Parke again, but he wanted to be as informal as possible. Cusack did not believe Parke had anything to do with the murder, but he could be someone who possessed valuable information that he was not sharing out of an over-abundance of caution.

Rather than arranging a meeting, the chief deliberately timed his visit to coincide with lunchtime Monday, when Charles Parke would likely be free.

Ed's business, The Buffalo Envelope Co. Photo from the Collection of The Buffalo History Museum. General photograph collection, Buildings - Factories - Paper.

Cusack's plan worked perfectly. He entered the office just as Parke was pulling on his overcoat. Burdick's business partner paused in surprise.

"Chief Cusack! To what do I owe the pleasure?"

"Oh, just some routine follow-up work. I want to look at Mr. Burdick's things, if you can point me in the direction."

"Of course, of course," Parke replied pleasantly. "Please come this way." He led the chief across the room to a spotless desk.

"You've cleaned out Mr. Burdick's desk already," Cusack observed.

"Oh no, I hadn't thought what to do with Ed's things yet," Parke replied. "This is just how Ed left it last Thursday. Ed always cleaned everything from the surface of his desk before he left for the day."

Cusack tried to open the door, but it was locked. Parke noticed the difficulty. "If you'll wait just a moment, we have a master key. I'll find it so you can open the drawers and see the contents."

Parke returned and handed the key to Cusack. Ed's friend stood watching as the chief skimmed the contents of the drawer. He saw at once there was nothing of interest there, but he prolonged his search to talk with Parke.

"How is the investigation?" Parke asked. "Are you any closer to finding the scoundrel who killed Ed?"

"Yes, I think so," Cusack declared, with much more conviction than he felt. He watched to see the impact on Parke, but it was just what he expected in an innocent man: Parke looked pleased. "There are a few details I'd like to learn about to seal the case, but I don't see anything here."

"Is it anything I can help with?" Parke inquired.

"Well, the murderer had gone through Mr. Burdick's desk in his den, looking for something. It was the only thing that was disturbed in the room. We don't know what he was looking for."

Parke considered. "If Mr. Pennell is the killer—and I believe wholeheartedly that he is—he was probably looking for the records the detective gave Edwin."

"What records are those?"

"It was basically a log of all the detective had seen when he shadowed Mrs. Burdick, any time and place she met Mr. Pennell."

"Did you see these records yourself, Mr. Parke?"

"No," Parke shook his head. "Ed mentioned them in passing. I don't know where they are, but I assumed he kept them at home in his den."

Cusack stood. "Well, thank you again for your time, Mr. Parke. This has been helpful."

"Not at all," Parke said. "Ed was a good man. I want to help bring his killer to justice."

The chief paused at the door. "You say you are confident Arthur Pennell is behind this?"

Parke nodded. "Indeed, I am."

"But you say Mr. Burdick told you he wasn't afraid of Pennell."

Parke hesitated. "Well, he said Mr. Pennell would be a coward in a fair fight. But I think he worried he might attack him in a cowardly way. You know, shooting him in the back or something of that nature. This was only my impression, mind."

Cusack thanked him and departed.

Alfred Brookman tended furnaces for the Burdicks and other families in the area. The detectives interviewed him almost as an afterthought, but he surprised them by providing an important piece of information.

Brookman said Mr. Burdick hired him to keep the furnace working. "He'd hurt his hand someways and needed the help," he explained. He had been at the Burdick home a few days before the murder, and Ed told him he was fully recovered and would see to the furnace himself from now on.

Brookman had been at the neighbor's home Friday morning to tend to their furnace when he heard Katie Koenig call to him from an upstairs window at the Burdick home.

"What time was that?" Detective Sullivan demanded.

Brookman shrugged. "Along about 7:30, I'd guess." Katie ran outside and told him that Burdick was ill. She said the house was cold and asked if he could tend to the furnace. Alfred agreed to come by after he finished his work at the neighbor's home.

"I didn't get done there until later, so I never arrived at the Burdick place until nearly 10. When I got down to the furnace, it was very low. Katie said she put a shovelful of coal on it, but it didn't look like it." He said it had taken him quite a while to get the furnace back in working order.

"Was there anything unusual that you noticed down in the cellar, besides how low the furnace was?" Holmlund asked.

"No," Brookman said.

"Didn't see anything at all out of place or unusual?"

Brookman considered. "The only thing that was different was Mrs. Hull come down there with that man and was talking to him."

"What's that?" Sullivan asked sharply.

"I was almost finished when I heard someone come into the cellar by the inside stairs. They talked down there for a few minutes."

"You say it was Mrs. Hull and another person. Do you know who?"

"Well, I thought it was the doctor."

"Dr. Marcy?" Sullivan asked. "Did you recognize him?"

"No," Alfred replied. "I just supposed it was him because I was told Mr. Burdick was sick, see? I figured him and Mrs. Hull come down to get a look at the plumbing to see if it was sanitary. But I don't know who he was."

The detectives exchanged a glance. "Could you hear what they were saying?"

"I didn't pay no attention," Brookman replied.

"Did they know you were down there, Alfred?"

"They didn't at first. But when I finally got the furnace going, I put down the shovel and it rang out with a real sharp noise on the bricks, and scared the man.

"He called out, 'Who's there?' Mrs. Hull says, 'That is only the man who takes care of the furnace.' And I leaned out and said, 'It's me, it's Alfred.'"

"Did you get a good look at them?" Detective Holmlund asked.

Alfred said he hadn't. When Holmlund pressed him, he shook his head. He wouldn't recognize the man, if he saw him again.

"Well, but you'd recognize his voice?"

Brookman shook his head. "No, sir. He talked real low. I wouldn't know his voice." XXVIII

Holmlund looked skeptical. "Well, how sure are you that it was Mrs. Hull?"

"I'm positive it was her."

"Did they leave at once after you spoke?"

Alfred frowned, trying to remember. "No, but they wasn't there much longer. They talked low for a moment more and then went back upstairs."

The detectives saw they had gotten all they could from Alfred. They believed his story and assumed Mrs. Hull must have been talking with Dr. Marcy in the cellar, since he and Alfred were the only men known to be in the Burdick home that morning before the police arrived.

Sullivan and Holmlund discussed Alfred's information as they walked back to the station. Based on the estimates Alfred provided, the detectives theorized Mrs. Hull and Dr. Marcy must have gone to the cellar during the window of time after Dr. Howland called the police to report the murder and before the police arrived to investigate.

The detectives may have thought it was a little strange for Mrs. Hull to bring the doctor down to the cellar for a conference, but it could easily be attributed to a desire to protect the children from overhearing the dreadful details of their father's murder. However, her failure to mention the conversation in the cellar, even when providing a detailed description of all she had said and done that morning, aroused their suspicions.

Alfred's description of what he had seen in the cellar gave them the impression the man with Mrs. Hull was nervous. And Dr. Marcy's mysterious interference with the investigation had never been explained to the satisfaction of the police.

At the station, they briefed Chief Cusack on what they learned.

The chief listened intently. Alfred Brookman's account strengthened his suspicion that Mrs. Hull knew more about her son-in-law's murder than she admitted. Cusack was sure Dr. Marcy was not involved in Ed Burdick's murder, but he was equally confident that the doctor had shielded Mrs. Hull from police questioning. But why?

Brookman's story could prove critical to the investigation, and the chief commended the detectives for their work. They would give the information to DA Coatsworth, while the detectives focused on unearthing new leads and interviewing those who might be able to shed light on the crime.

A Talk with Gertrude Paine

On Wednesday, March 4, the police conducted their long-awaited interview with Mrs. Gertrude Paine. Chief Cusack and Detective Holmlund arrived at 492 Elmwood Avenue promptly at 7:30 p.m. They had arranged to interview Mrs. Paine in her home to inconvenience her as little as possible. Their knock was answered by Adolph Carlson, who grinned at Detective Holmlund and led them to the parlor.

Gertrude Paine was waiting in her parlor. She thanked Carlson and stood up to greet Cusack and Holmlund then gestured graciously to the deep plush sofas. "Please sit down, gentlemen, and help yourselves to coffee."

Mrs. Paine was well-known amongst the Elmwood Avenue set and admired for her beautiful, dramatic clothing and delicate manners. That evening, she wore a flowing silver gown and a heavy necklace. After exchanging a few pleasantries with their hostess, Detective Holmlund turned the conversation to their purpose.

"Could you tell us when you last spoke to Mr. Burdick?"

"Thursday afternoon," Gertrude replied. "I telephoned him at his office."

"For what purpose?"

"He had asked me to—find out some information for him." Gertrude hesitated and then added, "He wanted to know whether the Pennells were going to attend a dance at the Elmwood Dance Club. He wanted to go but did not want to take the chance of encountering either of them."

"I told him I would ask Mrs. Pennell if I saw her."

"And were they planning to be there?" the detective asked.

"I did not see Mrs. Pennell, so I wanted to let Mr. Burdick know that I had not been able to learn whether they would be there."

The police asked about Ed's demeanor and whether anything unusual stood out to her.

"Nothing whatever."

Chief Cusack turned the conversation to the murder. "Mrs. Paine, you know that we found your photograph in Mr. Burdick's den—"

"There is nothing unusual in that!" Gertrude cried. "It's customary for society people to exchange photographs."

Cusack replied in a soothing tone, "It merely gave me the impression that you are a close friend of Mr. Burdick's who might be able to shed light upon the case." This wasn't exactly true, but he hoped to ease Mrs. Paine's evident defensiveness.

Mrs. Paine appeared somewhat mollified, but her guarded demeanor did not change.

"Why don't you tell us about the night of the murder so we can better understand where you might help us," the chief suggested.

Mrs. Paine said she was at home the night of the murder, playing with her small daughter. Her boarders, Mr. Carlson and Miss Hutchinson, were home and could attest to her whereabouts. She did not go out after dinner.

"Were you aware of Mr. Burdick's marital problems, Mrs. Paine?" Detective Holmlund asked.

Gertrude nodded. "Yes, everyone knew."

"Do you know how Mr. Burdick discovered the relations between his wife and Mr. Pennell?"

"I believe Mrs. Pennell first told Mr. Burdick what was happening in regard to Mr. Pennell and Mrs. Burdick."

"You say Mrs. Pennell told Mr. Burdick about the relationship," Cusack repeated. Gertrude nodded. "Do you know why she did so? Did she want him to intervene and put a stop to it?"

Gertrude Paine shook her head. "It's a mystery to me why she ever said anything to him." She frowned slightly. "I know that later, she was upset that Ed planned to divorce Allie."

"Had Mrs. Pennell spoken to her husband?"

"I don't know," Mrs. Paine replied. "She never told me directly about the relations between them, and I could not ask." Cusack pressed her on this, and Gertrude shook her head impatiently. "I don't mean that we never discussed it, but Mrs. Pennell never told me directly about the affair. She did say she had been coaxing Ed to take his wife back."

"And what did Mr. Burdick say to this?"

"He wouldn't have her," Gertrude said. "He'd taken her back before, several times in fact, but she continued to meet Mr. Pennell. He—Mr. Burdick—told me that Mrs. Pennell had started the trouble, and she could not intercede to erase it now."

"What was Mr. Burdick's state of mind, do you think?" Holmlund asked.

Detective John Holmlund

"Well—he resented Mr. Pennell coming into his house as a friend and then breaking up his home, of course. Mr. Burdick and Mr. Pennell used to golf together. Mr. Pennell had agreed to leave the city two years ago, but then he never did."

"Did you see Mr. Burdick often?"[XII]

"No," Mrs. Paine said sharply. "I met him a few times after Allie left. I was a friend to him." After a moment, she added, "We also had some business."

"What business?" Cusack asked.

Gertrude Paine's face reddened. She admitted she had borrowed some money from Burdick, but insisted, "It was a loan, not a gift."

"Mrs. Paine, we do not wish to pry, but we need to understand the circumstances of all dealings with Burdick to solve this case. Can you please tell us the details of this loan?"

"I purchased some new home furnishings on credit," Mrs. Paine replied. Her facial expression did not noticeably change, but her tone was resentful. "What we had was scarcely decent."

"And the bill came due, and you appealed to Mr. Burdick for the loan?"

She nodded unwillingly. "There was nothing improper about it," she said emphatically. "It's hardly unusual."

When Cusack and Holmlund persisted by asking her follow-up questions about the amount of money she borrowed and whether her husband was aware of the loan, Mrs. Paine said icily, "I don't see the bearing of this information on the case. Am I obliged to answer?"

"Not at present," Chief Cusack replied. His answer hung in the air for several seconds.

Before speaking, Mrs. Paine took a sip of water and smoothed an imaginary wrinkle in her dress. "My relationship to Mr. Burdick was purely social, if that is what you're asking. I was a friend to him, and he to me. Nothing more."

"Did Burdick confide in you about his troubles?"

Gertrude said he had. "He told me the rumors about Allie were true. He said he had the proof necessary to obtain a divorce." Mrs. Paine admitted to sharing information about the Pennells from time to time with Ed. "About two and a half weeks ago, I spoke to Carrie, er, to Mrs. Pennell. She asked me if I had heard any rumor that she and Arthur were divorcing."

"I said I'd heard the rumor. Mrs. Pennell told me she never had such an idea. She didn't know that such a rumor was in circulation until she and Mr. Pennell returned from the Waldorf Astoria, and someone asked her about it."

"And was Mrs. Pennell upset?" Detective Holmlund asked. "What did she say after you told her you heard the story?"

According to Gertrude, Carrie Pennell was calm but said in no uncertain terms that she had no intention of divorcing Arthur.

Mrs. Paine said she had met Ed Burdick a few times since Alice left Buffalo in early December of the previous year. Once at a candy store, and two or three times at J.H. Adams store. They had dinner downtown one evening at a restaurant on Main street.

"Did you ever go to his home?"

"Yes, but not alone," Mrs. Paine answered. "I've only been to the Burdick home in my husband's company."

"Why did you arrange to meet at shops, instead of going to Mr. Burdick's office or home?"

"I did not wish to invite the impression that there was anything improper," she said coldly.

Cusack nodded, attempting to smooth her ruffled feathers. "People do talk," he sympathized. "Even when it's all above board."

"It was not only that. Mr. Burdick knew people were following him. Mr. Pennell had hired private detectives, and they trailed him."

"Did Mr. Burdick tell you that?" Cusack demanded.

"Yes, of course. He said Mr. Pennell was having him followed. He said, 'They will have a hard time earning their money.'"

"So, you took care not to visit his house because of the way your presence there might be framed. Did he ever visit you in your home?"

She said Ed had called at her home with Allie. "Or if Mrs. Warren was here," she added. Mrs. Warren, she explained, was a mutual friend. "Ed greatly admires her."

"Did Mr. Burdick perhaps have some additional interest in Mrs. Warren?" Holmlund hinted.

Gertrude did not answer directly. Instead, she said when she met Ed for dinner in January, he told her excitedly that Mrs. Warren was going to get her divorce. "I said nothing to Mr. Burdick, of course," she told the officers. "But—I shouldn't be surprised to learn soon that Mrs. Warren is engaged to another man."

"Mrs. Warren is engaged?"

"I did not say that," Mrs. Paine said. "I only say I wouldn't be surprised to learn of an engagement."

Cusack's ears pricked up. "Couldn't that other man perhaps have been Mr. Burdick?"

Mrs. Paine lifted an eyebrow. "I don't know of any engagement between Mrs. Warren and Mr. Burdick. I would be very surprised if that had been the case." She yawned conspicuously. "It is almost time to tuck my daughter in for the night," she told them.

Cusack and Holmlund took the hint and rose. They thanked Mrs. Paine for her time and, before he left, Cusack informed her the police would probably return to ask more questions in the coming days.

Back outside, Cusack and Holmlund conferred in low voices. Their impression of Gertrude Paine was mixed. She was attractive and charming, but there was an element of cattiness to her. Her love of status and the finer things in life was evident. She did not have disposable income, but her lack of money did not prevent her from spending lavishly.

Mrs. Paine's unwillingness to state how much money she owed Ed Burdick and whether her husband knew she was in debt to him caused both men to believe her debts were significant. Her relationship with Mr. Burdick seemed to be one of financial dependence, but based on what they had learned so far, it was unlikely Ed would have exploited the situation in any way.

"Did you notice how things were arranged?" Detective Holmlund mused. "With the coffee pot and cups already out?"

Cusack looked interested and the detective continued. "Mrs. Paine takes in boarders to make ends meet. She does not have servants, but she did not want us to know it."

Recognition dawned in Cusack's eyes. "She had the coffee out so she could offer us something without having to go and get it—"

"…and show there was no servant to do it," Holmlund finished.

"That is very clever," Cusack told Holmlund admiringly. "She didn't answer the door herself, either, did she?"

"No. And if I had not been here a few days ago, I would have thought Carlson worked for her, even," Holmlund said thoughtfully. The chief nodded. Mrs. Paine certainly had a talent for creating a particular impression.

Part 3

Becalmed

For about a week after the murder, the police were besieged with updates.

The medical examiner's office positively identified Ed's putter as the murder weapon. Close examination revealed the golf club had been wiped down but still had some tiny blood and brain matter particles on it.

With that, a large piece of Cusack's jigsaw puzzle fell into place. Unfortunately, it showed the frame he had constructed around the crime was not right. In the first days of the investigation, the frame that the chief constructed fit a desperate, wicked woman who came to Ed Burdick's house by appointment, for the purpose of killing him. She presented herself as a friend, but she planned the attack, brought the weapon with her, and took it away again when she left.

Now that they knew one of Ed's golf clubs had been used to kill him, everything was called into question. A golf club in Burdick's den was a weapon of opportunity. If the murderer arrived on the scene with no weapon, then it was probable that the crime was not pre-meditated after all. That introduced many new scenarios. Perhaps a woman had gone to Burdick to plead with him, they argued, and she flew into a rage and struck Ed.

> The Burdick case, like photographic paper, gets darker the more it is exposed. —The Atlanta Journal.

The newspapers reflected the confusion the investigators felt.

In the most popular emerging theory in the press, a married woman had an appointment with Burdick at his home Thursday night. Her suspicious husband followed her there and killed Ed in a blind rage. The woman's silence would be assured, both for the safety of her husband and to avoid being mixed up in a socially ruinous scandal. XXVII

At least one potentially jealous husband had been ruled out: J.B. Warren, the ex-husband of Ed's love interest, Helen Warren. His company confirmed he was traveling near St. Louis at the time of the murder. The police checked with the hotels where he had stayed and confirmed he was in Missouri when Ed was killed.

Holmlund and Sullivan worked the Burdick case full-time, but the other detectives on the police force occasionally assisted them. Detective Cornish had taken a second look at Ed Burdick's clothing, which the police had taken away as evidence from the crime scene. The clothes, with the exception of the undershirt, were clean and unbloodied. Cornish, however, noticed some barely perceptible bloodstains on the inner waist and right leg of the drawers, and pointed them out. This indicated the murderer pulled them off of the victim, after the initial strike.

When the police leads began to dry up, a flood of false confessions and unsolicited advice addressed to Chief Cusack took their place.

Some of the letters were eerie, and others were amusing. *You want to know who killed Burdick? I did it. Burdick was lying on his couch when I struck him. He only let one groan out of him. It was about time that such a man was put out of the way! Goodbye till we never meet again.*

Several anonymous letters named particular persons as the murderer. Investigation invariably revealed no links between the person named and the crime, and the letters were thought to be the work of someone motivated by a personal grudge.

Many letters demanded a reward in exchange for the name of the murderer and more than a few claimed to have seen the murderer's face in their dreams. A clairvoyant offered this helpful tip: *The party you are looking for is a woman, dressed as a man.*

Chief Cusack's favorite letter advised the police to photograph Burdick's eyes with strong lenses. *If Burdick could see his murderer as he was dying, the murderer's face will be in the pupil of his eye and can be photographed after death.* XII

All kinds of theories were advanced, all of which seemed as likely as anything else to have happened.

Without any concrete new information, the best hope police had of identifying the murderer, beyond a confession, was locating one of the missing items and tracing it back to the murderer.

There were three missing items: the bottle of pre-mixed cocktails, the detective's records, and Ed's gold watch. The missing bottle was almost a hopeless quest. The police had no doubt it had existed, and it was odd that Ed had purchased something he would not drink. Nevertheless, its importance was debatable. Even if it could be found, they now knew it was not the murder weapon. The medical examiner found no evidence of poison in the cocktail mixture. At most, the bottle might have told them something about an anticipated guest.

The police were more enthusiastic about the detective's records and the gold watch.

Detective Sullivan decided to interview Detective Boland, the private sleuth Ed had hired to gather information about Alice's affair with Arthur Pennell. The police had paid little attention when he was interviewed by the newspaper, but with little progress made on the case, Sullivan was willing to travel to New York City to talk to him.

Detective Sullivan interviewed the detective Ed hired to gather evidence against Alice.

John Boland confirmed he had shadowed Alice and Pennell for quite a while and gave Sullivan a summary of their meetings in and around Buffalo. Boland let Sullivan review his records, which he had used to compile the log he gave to Mr. Burdick.

"Do you know what Mr. Burdick did with the records you gave to him?"

"If he did not keep them, I presume he handed them over to this lawyer," Boland said.

Sullivan agreed, and his next visit was to George Miller, Ed's divorce attorney. "The detective's records!" Miller exclaimed. "Of course, I am familiar with them. They are—they were the cornerstone of the divorce suit."

Sullivan asked for the records, and the attorney looked startled. "I don't have charge of them. I requested that Mr. Burdick bring them when we had an appointment, but he always took them away again."

"But where did he keep them?" Sullivan persisted.

Miller scratched his head. "Well, I don't know. Mr. Burdick was careful with those records. I assume he kept them under lock and key somewhere. He was relying upon them to secure his divorce."

Ed's home and office had been thoroughly searched, and the police knew that if the records were in either place, they would have found them. Sullivan doubted that Ed had another secret hiding place, and he suspected the murderer stole them after killing Burdick and destroyed them at once.

Detective Holmlund, meanwhile, searched for the pocket watch. It was a distinctive, heavy gold piece, inscribed with the owner's initials. He first visited the shop where the watch was purchased.

"Oh yes," the jeweler said. "I know the piece well. Mr. Burdick would bring it in to be reset now and then."

"You don't have it now?" Holmlund asked.

"No, sir, I haven't seen it since he last brought it in, perhaps two months ago."

After the luckless visit to the jeweler, Detective Holmlund went to every pawn shop in the vicinity, but no one had seen the watch.

When the police came up empty-handed in their search for the missing items, Cusack, Sullivan, and Holmlund returned to the list of suspects to dig further into their backgrounds. Though they were certain a woman was the killer, or at the very least an accessory to the crime, the chief was too cautious to rule out Arthur Pennell entirely. The other suspects were Mrs. Pennell, Mrs. Hull, and Mrs. Paine.

The police turned to Arthur Pennell's known movements before and after the murder. Mr. Babcock confirmed that on Thursday evening, the night before the murder, Pennell had come into the garage sometime after dinner to check if the maintenance on his car was finished. Mrs. Pennell supported her husband's claim that they sat together downstairs until he went to bed about 10:00 p.m.

According to the Pennells' maid, Lizzie, Arthur rose about 8:00 a.m. on the day of the murder, right about the time Burdick's body was discovered. Pennell had breakfast at 8:30 a.m. According to Lizzie and Henry Orrett, the man who tended the furnace, Mr. Pennell's demeanor was in every way normal.

At 10:00 a.m., Pennell visited Walbridge's and asked for a cheap replacement for a gun he purchased three weeks earlier, saying the first had been stolen. The police spoke to E.W. Fox, the clerk who sold both weapons to Pennell. The first gun was a .32 Smith & Wesson revolver that cost nearly $12, and Pennell had taken his time when he selected it. When he came in on February 27, news of Ed Burdick's murder had not yet circulated around town, but Fox said Pennell seemed hurried and out-of-sorts that morning. He asked for a cheap gun, and Fox suggested an Iver Johnson revolver for five dollars. Pennell did not handle the gun. He merely glanced at it and agreed to purchase it. That was atypical behavior from Mr. Pennell, who was a regular customer and usually very pleasant.

From there, Arthur Pennell went to the Iroquois barbershop. "Mr. Pennell came into the barbershop at 10:45 a.m. that morning," George Wood told police. Wood had been Pennell's barber for years, and he said Pennell came in daily between 10:30–11:15. "I shaved him. He did not get a haircut, but he asked me to trim the front of his hair in one or two places, which I did. He got out of the chair at 11:05."

The barber refuted the idea that Pennell seemed hurried or agitated. "His manner and demeanor were as usual. It so happened that while I was shaving him, I mentioned the divorce affair to him, as on previous occasions he had mentioned it to me. He spoke of it without the slightest sign of excitement or of agitation. In his usual quiet way, he remarked that there was nothing new in it, that it is simply going along. He evinced no haste and was not in any hurry and was not flustered. He got out of the chair leisurely and went out of the shop at about 11:10." xxix

Despite the hardware clerk's assertion that Pennell seemed disturbed in some way, the police believed that Arthur's alibi checked out.

The only new thing they had learned was that Pennell was in New York City the Tuesday before the murder. Arthur traveled so often that the police did not believe this was a significant detail until they learned that Alice Burdick had met him there, ostensibly to discuss the divorce, and while there, she sent a telegram to her mother in Buffalo. This was unusual. Telegrams were expensive, and Alice only contacted her mother that way when the matter was urgent. She received a response from her mother within a short time. At that point, she had gone back to Atlantic City, while Arthur took the night train back to Buffalo.

The detectives wanted to know what the telegrams contained. Alice said she remembered sending a telegram to ask if her mother was feeling well. She had not heard from her in several days and was concerned. The detectives then requested Alice provide the telegrams to them. She said she didn't have a copy of the one she sent, and she destroyed the response from her mother. "I never keep communications," she told the police.

When detectives questioned Mrs. Hull, she said the telegrams had actually been sent two weeks before Ed's murder. She did not show the telegram to the police and claimed to have mislaid or thrown it away. Undeterred, the police filed a request with Western Union Telegraph Company requesting copies of the telegrams between Mrs. Hull and Mrs. Burdick. After two days, the company responded. They were unable to retrieve copies of the telegrams. Another clue evaporated.

The police detected two possible motives Mrs. Hull may have had for murdering her son-in-law. She may have fiercely resented Ed for banishing her daughter, and she may have been worried about her own future. She had no money, and if Ed Burdick remarried, what was she to do? Her behavior the morning of the murder was peculiar, and she had shown no emotion after discovering Ed's brutal slaying. Contradicting all of this was Dr. Marcy's assurance that Mrs. Hull was frail and her reputed friendliness with Burdick.

Carrie Pennell had a powerful motive for killing Ed Burdick, even if it wasn't immediately obvious. Alice Burdick openly shared her expectation that Pennell would divorce his wife to be with her and save her from social disgrace. Alice had no money of her own, so she would also look to Arthur for financial support to supplement any alimony she collected.

Mrs. Pennell made it clear she did not want a divorce from her husband, but if the Burdicks divorced, it was far more likely Arthur would leave her to rescue Alice. Carrie had pleaded with Ed several times to take Alice back. It wasn't outside the realm of possibility to imagine she had gone to his home late at night to make a final appeal to him. She wanted the Burdicks' marriage to remain intact, but if Ed was unwilling, then perhaps the next best thing would be if Alice were a widow. At least she would not be in financial straits, nor would she face the stigma of being a divorcée—and that would relieve the pressure on Arthur to marry her.

The police traced Mrs. Pennell's whereabouts on the day before the murder and the time immediately afterward. She had been to a community meeting the day before the murder. That evening, the Pennells' maid, Lizzie Romance, verified Mrs. Pennell was home and had gone to bed shortly after her husband. Arthur Pennell had also confirmed this.

Carrie Pennell had breakfasted with her husband Friday morning. In the afternoon, she visited a friend and stayed for tea. She learned of Ed's murder while in her friend's company. The problem for Arthur and Carrie Pennell was that they were each other's alibi at the time the murder was actually committed in the early morning hours of February 27.

Alice Burdick had the strongest motive to kill her husband. She stood to lose nearly everything since the divorce courts were sure to be more sympathetic toward Ed. Alice would be hurt financially, her daughters would be shamed, her mother would be potentially left homeless, and she, Alice, would be disgraced. The police had not focused on her because she did not have the opportunity to do it. Mrs. Burdick had been seen reading in a common area of Hotel Traymore until late on the night of the murder, and the police were already familiar with her train trip back to Buffalo.

The only realistic way Alice could have been involved in Ed's death was by asking someone else to do it.

Mrs. Paine could be considered a suspect, but she was not a likely culprit. The social status and luxuries, so dear to Mrs. Paine's heart, would be threatened if Ed Burdick demanded repayment or refused to loan her more money, but Burdick had no reason to call in his debts, and no evidence suggested he had. It was possible Gertrude Paine had gone to see Burdick late at night if she were having an affair with him, but this too, seemed highly unlikely.

Chief Cusack suddenly remembered Dr. Paine's remark, quoted in the paper, that if Mrs. Paine went out at 1 a.m., he would not even ask where she was going. He grinned. Dr. Paine might not ask his wife where she was going at one o'clock in the morning, but he would certainly follow her. However, the detectives had verified Dr. Paine was in Batavia on Thursday and Friday, which ruled him out.

As it turned out, Mrs. Paine's movements were fairly easy to verify. The police were able to confirm her whereabouts before and after the murder. At the actual time of Ed's death, she was sleeping. This satisfied Chief Cusack that she was not involved, and he directed Sullivan and Holmlund to focus their efforts on the other suspects.

As the days passed, the police chafed under the continual questions and requests for updates from the press and the public. The detectives were diligently working the case with nothing to show for it. After the terrific storm caused by Ed's murder, the investigation now found itself lost at sea, becalmed in waters as still as a mill pond.

Deluge

Arthur Pennell grew increasingly rattled in the days after Ed's murder. The conversations with the police, the attention from the media, and the way people eyed him wherever he went preyed upon his nerves.

On Friday, March 6, Arthur arrived at his office in the Austin Building at 110 Franklin Street at his usual time. Unlike most legal offices in the city, Arthur's office was spacious with an abundance of natural light.

The building had a storied history. Before it was converted to office space, it had been home to a Universalist church where no less than three US presidents had prayed: John Quincy Adams, Millard Fillmore, and Abraham Lincoln. Now Arthur Pennell turned to the airy, elegant building for sanctuary.

The Austin Building
Image courtesy of Buffaloah.com

He had accomplished very little over the past two weeks. Several cases were awaiting action, but Arthur could not concentrate on his work. After several failed attempts to draft a brief, he put the case folder aside and pulled some blank paper from the drawer. He began to write, rapidly covering two pages with fluid handwriting.

His letter, addressed to a friend in Pottsville, Pennsylvania, read as follows:

> *I presume you have seen the newspaper accounts of a mysterious crime here at Buffalo, in which my name has most unjustly received great publicity. In the mass of sensationalism and yellow journalism which has followed the affair, the truth was utterly lost.*
>
> *I had no connection with the crime. My name was brought in through the divorce proceedings which were then pending. There was no truth in the charges in those proceedings. They were absolutely denied under oath by the defendant and myself. I was dragged in out of vindictiveness because my wife and myself had taken the part of the wife against the husband and she had come to me for legal advice and protection.*
>
> *The man in the case was all the time in intimate relations with other women. The case would have been quickly tried and the charges disproved, but just at this time and at the most unfortunate time, occurred his death at the hands of some unknown woman, and the whole matter became public.*
>
> *Then came a deluge of lies and falsehoods which had no basis in fact. The notoriety has been almost unbearable. I want you and some of my friends I care about to have the truth, and I know that you will believe in me. I have been very much broken up over it all.*
>
> A.R. PENNELL

Many of Pennell's statements in the letter must be regarded as false, but some of them might have been true. One statement was undeniable, which was his feeling about the scrutiny to which he was subjected. *The notoriety has been almost unbearable*. Feeling a little relieved after venting his feelings, the young attorney posted his letter and boarded a streetcar, bound for Elmwood Avenue. According to all who knew him, Arthur Pennell was a sensitive person who was deeply concerned with what others thought and said about him. The harsh spotlight of attention that now shone on him would have distressed a much more hardened character than he. And, worst of all, the fears he had long ago voiced to Alice Burdick that his letters to her would be found and made public seemed to be on the brink of manifesting.

He avoided going out all weekend. He stayed home and attempted to read. The gloom and uncertainty that pervaded the previous week did not abate as the new week began. The inquest into the murder of Edwin Burdick was scheduled to begin Saturday, March 14. Arthur's anxiety was evident.

The next day, March 10, cold rain soaked the city of Buffalo. The murder was still the only topic of conversation, and speculation was running rampant.

When Arthur arrived at the Iroquois barbershop midmorning, George was cutting another man's hair. He looked up to greet Arthur, and the scissors stopped, mid-snip. "Why, Mr. Pennell!" he exclaimed. "Are you unwell?"

Arthur assured the barber he was fine. When George beckoned to him a few minutes later, he sank into the chair and stared at his reflection in the mirror. No wonder George had been shocked by his appearance. The dark crescents beneath his eyes and his excessive pallor declared to all who saw him that he was a soul in torment.

He realized George was talking to him. "A man must eat well and sleep well to—"

"George, I am in a bad situation," Arthur interrupted. Suddenly, he wanted to tell someone of his worries. It would purge them from his spirit. But, ever cautious, he spoke low so only George could hear him. "If I were a detective figuring this case out, I would be the first one to accuse myself, I believe! Everything seems to point to me. I have been with Mrs. Burdick a good deal, and I was named as the corespondent. I'm the only man, so far as anyone knows, who has had any trouble with Burdick." XII

"But, you're not—"

"No, no, I'm not," Arthur broke in, speaking feverishly. "But no matter whether I am arrested or not, I shall always be pointed out as the man who killed Burdick. Everything seems to implicate me."

He broke off, then added bitterly, "I cannot say I blame the police or the newspapers for speaking of me as they do." This was no doubt an accurate summation of the newspaper coverage, in Arthur's opinion. However, the newspapers had largely accepted the police assertion that a woman had murdered Burdick. His name appeared in every column, due to the public's interest in his affair with Alice.

"But I had absolutely nothing to do with the killing of Ed Burdick!" Pennell continued. He looked at George pleadingly. "He and I were not the best of friends, to be sure, but I never would have harmed a hair on his head." xxx

"No, I'm sure you wouldn't, Mr. Pennell," George said soothingly. "Everyone who knows you knows this to be the fact. I'd take my oath on it."

When George finished, Arthur Pennell rose and thanked him. He paid his bill and wandered out, disregarding the heavy rain pouring down.

Arthur Pennell, circa 1902

At three o'clock, a reporter came to his office. Arthur unwisely agreed to speak to him, but he did not anticipate how aggressive the reporter would be. It is not difficult to imagine the panic he felt when the reporter began to question him about his recent letter to his friend in Pennsylvania.

"What was your idea, Mr. Pennell, in stating in your letter to your friend in Pennsylvania that Mr. Burdick was killed by some unknown woman? On what theory or fact was that based?"

Arthur visibly flinched. "I have not stated that I wrote that letter," he said.

The reporter looked at him incredulously. "Do you deny it? We have proof you did write it."

After a moment, Arthur replied, "I don't deny it, but I decline to discuss it."

"You think the murder might be the result of a conspiracy?"

"It might—"

"Might it not have been partially the work of a woman whose feelings had been played upon? Perhaps a woman who had been prevailed upon to deliberately admit a man to the house who committed the murder?"

Here the reporter noted that "Mr. Pennell became greatly agitated; his hands trembled violently. Instead of the customary calm, almost cynical expression of his face, there was one that bespoke interest, to say the least."

However, the interviewee was careful to remain noncommittal. "I suppose it's possible," was all he would say.

The reporter told Pennell of a messenger boy who saw a strange man, believed to be the murderer, in front of the Burdick home. "He says he can identify the man if he sees him again."

"I wasn't aware of that."

The reporter, seeing Pennell would say no more about the potential witness, moved back to the topic in which he had shown more interest. "To return to the subject of the woman, you must have some grounds for mentioning her in your letter. What are they?"

"I haven't said I wrote that letter."

"Do you know of—or have you heard from any of yours or Burdick's friends—that he had improper relations with any woman?" the reporter demanded.

"No," Arthur answered simply.

"You asked Mr. Burdick to withdraw his suit for divorce, didn't you?"

Arthur froze, and after a moment he said softly, "I cannot discuss that."

"Have you been reading about the murder in the papers?" the reporter asked. Pennell said he had. "As a man of the world, do you not think it peculiar that Burdick, if he had expected a woman to visit him, should have set out that particular food—tarts, cheese—found on the table."

"Nothing like that would have ever been offered to a visitor by a man like Burdick," Pennell stated flatly.

"Do you think it could have been a plant?"

"Oh yes," Arthur said, with some energy. "A thing put there to deceive. Yes, I do."

The reporter raised an eyebrow. "That's it, eh? Wouldn't that be the doing of, say, an older lady, whose idea of a nice snack might be a tart?"

"It's plausible," Arthur replied. He seemed to be considering the idea.

The reporter decided this was the right time to get to his real question. "Do you know that a woman, and a friend of Mrs. Burdick's, are under suspicion and the police say they are going to make an arrest within 48 hours?"

Arthur rose. "You must excuse me now. I cannot discuss this any further."

After the reporter was gone, Arthur sat down and passed a handkerchief over his perspiring face. It was time to go home.

The Valley of Sorrow

Arthur was home by 4:30 p.m. but found himself utterly unable to be calm.

Another reporter called his home and asked if he would be open to an interview. Without knowing why, Arthur agreed to talk with him that evening at 6:30 p.m.

He paced back and forth in the parlor, occasionally looking through the window at the dripping trees and darkening sky. A soft sound behind him caused him to whirl around, but it was only the maid emptying the ash tray.

"Lizzie, is Mrs. Pennell upstairs?"

"I believe so, sir," the young woman replied.

Arthur hurried up the steps and found his wife busily crocheting. "I'm going to go out," he told her. "Just to be out-of-doors for a little while. I am too restless. Driving will be a distraction."

Carrie Pennell looked at her husband. It had been nearly two weeks since the murder, and she knew he had not had a single moment's rest since then.

"I shall go with you," she said firmly. As she spoke, she rose and reached for her heaviest sweater. Arthur watched her quietly. Whether he had intended for his wife to accompany him or not, arguing the point with her was useless.

A drawing of Carrie Pennell

At 4:45 p.m., the Pennells climbed into their electric carriage, shrugging off the discomfort of riding in the rain. The carriage with its detachable top and the initials ARP stamped in red letters on the back was a novelty that attracted a lot of attention. Arthur loved to drive.

During their drive, the Pennells' behavior was peculiar. For 30 minutes, they drove up and down a single country road, at a pace so slow that a person walking could easily outpace them. They were conspicuous; several people noticed them.

They stopped at a saloon afterward, and Carrie waited outside while Arthur dashed inside to buy cigars. He chatted with the bartender for a few minutes until he overheard someone say it was after 5:30 p.m. He checked his watch hurriedly. "I didn't realize it was so late," he said. "We still have a drive ahead to get home."

Arthur paid for his cigars and two small glasses of whisky. A moment later, he emerged from the saloon carrying one of the glasses and handed it to his wife before getting into the carriage.

When they reached the outskirts of Buffalo, the carriage rolled to a stop. Arthur and Carrie got out and worked together to detach the top from the car. An outside observer certainly would have found it odd to see the stately Mrs. Pennell standing in the mud with the rain pelting down on her, helping to wrestle the detachable top off of an automobile. After a few moments' struggle, Arthur and Carrie Pennell climbed back into the carriage and drove on, now with nothing shielding them from the rain.

The automobile took off at a jump traveling down Kensington Road leading past the Jammerthal rock quarries. *Jammerthal* is a German word meaning "valley of sorrow."

A sudden gust of wind blew Arthur's hat off, attracting the attention of two small boys who were standing near the road. Arthur made a grab for it and missed. But the automobile swerved, and as they watched, the wheels of the carriage went over the curb. For a moment, the automobile was airborne, then it plunged down 30 feet, landing with a crash at the bottom of the quarry.

The boys who had witnessed the accident were frightened. They ran to the nearest house and alerted the family to what had happened. Ten minutes later, three men joined the boys. They carried a lantern with them and carefully climbed down into the quarry, taking care not to slide in the mud and fall onto the jagged rocks. At the bottom of the quarry, the wrecked auto was lying upside down. The rescuers seized some timbers and used them as levers to lift the 1,800-pound electric carriage. Beneath it lay the bodies of a man and a woman. They saw at once that the man was dead. The woman was unconscious, but a slight whimper told the men she was still alive. An ambulance soon came and took her to the nearest hospital.

Eleven days after Ed Burdick was murdered in his den, Arthur Pennell's lifeless body was carried out of the quarry.

That evening, Coatsworth came to the morgue with a young boy. Dr. Danser came out to greet them. He looked doubtfully at the boy but said nothing. If the district attorney wanted to bring a young boy to a morgue, he could do that.

"Dr. Danser, this is Herbert Martin," Coatsworth said. "He's a messenger who was working on Ashland Avenue the morning of the murder. He got a good look at a strange man near the Burdick house."

"Ah," Danser said. "I see."

"Herbert, this is Dr. Danser. He's one of our medical examiners." The boy shook hands politely.

"May we see the body, Dr. Danser?"

The medical examiner motioned them back. "Is he recognizable?" Coatsworth asked in a low voice.

Dr. Danser nodded. "Yes. It's the strangest thing. In appearance, his head looks just like Mr. Burdick's did. It's crushed in the back, but the face is intact." The doctor led them into a small room where the body laid on a table. He uncovered Pennell's face.

"Well, Herbert?" Coatsworth barked. "Is this the man you saw on Ashland Avenue in the early morning hours of February 27?"

"No sir," Herbert Martin said decidedly.

Coatsworth was visibly disappointed. He tried to conceal it, but he took on the appearance of a deflated balloon. "Are you sure, lad?"

"I am sure," the boy declared. "The man I saw was heavier. He looked rough. He wore rough clothes."

Coatsworth dismissed the boy. He paused a moment to talk to Dr. Danser. "Was there anything in Pennell's pockets?" he asked.

"Yes," Danser replied. "Nothing that will interest you I fear, but it's all here in this bin."

Coatsworth snatched the bin and pawed through its contents: a small monogrammed gold watch, two pen-knives, several keys, a handkerchief, and a wallet containing $35.

"What have we here?" Coatsworth's eyes lit up. He held up a bundle of newspaper clippings. "Got some extraordinary interest in the case, does he?"

Danser shook his head slightly. Coatsworth was poring over the clips, presumably looking for evidence showing Arthur was closely following the police investigation and panicking as he saw the detectives closing in on him. This was not the case.

Even if Arthur was the top suspect, his collection would have disappointed Coatsworth. Of nearly sixty clippings, not one related to the case. Most of the clippings were sentimental poetry peppered with a few love stories.

Cursing his bad luck, Coatsworth dropped the bin on the table and left the room. This was the highest profile case of his career, and two weeks later, he was still unable to name a suspect, even a dead one. He was anxious to have a suspect and to prosecute the case.

He came face-to-face with Chief Cusack in the hall and said hello. "Going to see Pennell?"

"Yes," Cusack said shortly. He was unenthusiastic about the DA. Coatsworth was 36 years old, aggressive, and ambitious. Cusack suspected the DA was more interested in advancing his career than serving justice or the residents of Erie County.

"Well, he's back there," Coatsworth said. "I'll be going."

Cusack entered the room and greeted Dr. Danser, who was writing a few notes. He looked sadly at Arthur's broken body. He had liked the young attorney.

"Should I give you his effects, Chief Cusack?" Danser asked.

"Yes, please." The chief held a clipping up and squinted at it while Danser stepped out to search for a bag the chief could use to carry Arthur's things.

> *Oh, I have wondered at the fearless heart,*
> *With which strong men and tender women*
> *Go to meet great death, but now I seem to know*

He picked up another and read it:

House and lands are gone for aye
Kith and kin like the wild wind flee
Life and breath have fluttered away
But love hath blossomed eternally

And another:

How be of Death afraid
When we have dared to Live

Dr. Danser returned with a bag and Cusack carefully deposited Arthur's belongings in it. He thanked the doctor and looked toward Arthur once more. He left the room a moment later, intent on getting back to the station. When he walked outside, he found Coatsworth was on the steps talking with a reporter. "Will the death of Attorney Pennell impact the investigation?"

"Decline to answer."

"Do you expect to make any arrests in the next 24 hours?"

"Decline to answer." [XXXI]

Cusack did not linger. He had no wish to speak to the press nor to speak with Coatsworth. "Chief Cusack!" a voice called. The chief ignored the shout and continued to walk briskly.

"Chief Cusack! Chief Cusack!" With a sigh, he looked up. The reporter who had been speaking to Coatsworth, a young man with short hair parted in the middle, hurried to his side. He held a small notepad in one hand and a grimy pencil in the other. "I have a few questions for you, sir."

Without waiting for Cusack to agree, he asked, "Was it an accident or suicide?"

"Indications point to it having been an accident," Chief Cusack replied.

"Do you not think there are reasons Pennell might have preferred death to life?"

"The man is dead now, I'm saying nothing."

"Will you say whether the police were in possession of any facts which might have been used to menace Pennell? Did he know the police might have certain facts?"

"I'm not a mind reader," Cusack retorted. "I don't know what Pennell might have thought or feared." XXXII

The reporter began to ask more questions, but Cusack shrugged him off irritably and headed back to the station.

The reporter did not appreciate the chief's response. The next day's paper quoted Cusack, with the following comment: "The convenient lack of knowledge regarding everything in connection with the case which was possessed by Chief Cusack was positively sublime." XXXII

Though the local paper had been unable to get a comment from Alice about Arthur Pennell's death, an intrepid reporter from *The San Francisco Examiner* did. The maid who answered his ring did not invite him in, but Alice consented to come to the door. When she appeared, the reporter asked, "Do you have any comment about the accident this afternoon, Mrs. Burdick?"

Alice looked puzzled. "What accident?"

The reporter took a breath. "Arthur Pennell was killed in an automobile accident this afternoon. His wife was with him, and she's not expected to survive."

Whatever the reporter expected, he was unprepared for Mrs. Burdick's blasé reaction.

"Is that so?" Alice said, in a tone of polite indifference. "We had not heard it." Her black, unfathomable eyes met the reporter's gaze squarely and gave no hint of internal suffering.

The reporter began to ask another question but Alice cut him off. "No, I have nothing to say." Just before the door shut, the reporter caught sight of Mrs. Hull standing silently in the background. XXXI

An Accident?

Arthur Pennell's body was released the next morning to the undertaker. Dr. Danser declared an autopsy unnecessary. There was not enough evidence to support the theory that Pennell had committed suicide, he said, adding that the death would be classified as accidental.

The Buffalo Enquirer dedicated its front page to covering the Pennell tragedy.

Though she survived the initial crash, doctors knew Carrie Pennell was unlikely to survive.

The newspaper alleged that Arthur Pennell was driven to suicide because the police were closing in on him. It described the meeting between Pennell and Alice in the city three days before the murder and the telegrams sent between Mrs. Burdick and her mother. "Following receipt of an answer to Mrs. Burdick's telegram, Pennell had taken a night train to Buffalo … [Ed Burdick, having] knowledge that the telegrams had passed between Mrs. Burdick in New York and Mrs. Hull here, was keenly anxious to know where Pennell was."

The last sentence was speculation. The police knew Burdick had asked Mrs. Paine to find out whether the Pennells were going to attend an upcoming dance, and it was possible his real aim was learning whether Pennell was in town. However, no one could confirm this.

The paper stated that the authorities had been unable to get the telegrams from Mrs. Burdick or Mrs. Hull. "But Pennell undoubtedly knew that the demand had been made so imperative that it had been referred to the general counsel of the Western Union Telegraph Company in New York City." XXXII

That evening, Carrie Pennell died without ever regaining consciousness.

A mourning wreath was placed on the Pennell's front door.

The Buffalo Enquirer reporter notified Gertrude Paine when they came to her house to request a comment.

"I can't believe it! Horrible!" the paper quoted Mrs. Paine as saying. When asked whether she thought the accident would help to solve the Burdick mystery, Mrs. Paine said sharply, "I do not. I don't believe the police are on the right track at all."

Police interviewed the Pennell's maid, Lizzie Romance, on the night of the accident. She told the police Mr. Pennell had an appointment to speak with two reporters at 6:30 p.m., and all the Pennells had taken with them on their ride was an umbrella. She did not believe the accident was deliberate.

Detective Holmlund asked if Lizzie knew anything about a burglary at the Pennell's home in January. The girl looked surprised and answered, "No."

"Mr. Pennell didn't mention a stolen gun to you?"

"No," Lizzie replied. There had been burglars in the house, but it was several months earlier. "But they were a queer kind of burglars. They did not steal any silverware or valuables of that kind. They simply rummaged through Mr. Pennell's papers, as if they were looking to find something in them. That is the only burglar I know of." [xxxix]

On March 13, three days after they plunged into the quarry, Arthur and Carrie were laid to rest side by side in Maine, in the Pennell family plot. A few close friends and family attended the service, and their request for privacy was respected. Alice Burdick was not present.

Speculation about the wreck that had killed the Pennells could not be muffled.

The friends and family of Arthur and Carrie, as well as Mr. Babcock, Pennell's mechanic, maintained the Pennells' wreck was accidental. Arthur—perhaps in the moment his hat flew off—had lost control of the machine, or perhaps made a false pull at the lever. They pointed to the slippery road that was so close to the precipice and how easily an auto could slide off the road.

Jammerthal Quarry on the day after the accident. The road the Pennells were traveling is on the right, and their wrecked electric carriage is visible in the lower left part of the picture.

Interestingly, Ed Burdick had recently told friends, "I do not think Pennell will live long. It would not surprise me to hear any day that he had committed suicide." XXXIII

On the following day, the newspapers came down on the same side of the argument. "Nearly everybody believes it was a deliberate suicide on the part of Pennell, and a determination to take his poor innocent wife with him into the hereafter. He had disgraced her, he probably felt, in being openly named as the corespondent in the divorce case, and he may not have had the heart to leave her behind to face the additional disgrace of being the widow of a suicide and a suspected murderer." XII

Reporters asked George Miller, Ed's attorney, whether Burdick's assessment of Pennell was true. Miller shifted in his chair and frowned. "Pennell could not recognize any blame attached to himself," he finally answered. "He didn't blame Burdick for feeling aggrieved at him. He admitted that it was the natural way for Burdick to feel. At the same time, he didn't feel that he had any cause to reproach himself. He seemed to feel that the situation was one which could not be prevented. Mrs. Burdick was dependent on him. He had tremendous influence over her ... he seemed to feel that their relations were the most natural thing in the world. Burdick despised him, but he never feared him." XXXIII

An interview with Mr. J.B. Warren was published in the newspaper. There had been much speculation about Mrs. Warren and the public was intensely interested in what her ex-husband had to say.

Mr. Warren was described as a young man who was about 28 years old, good-looking with an athletic build. Reporters described him as a likable person. However, when asked what he thought of the crime, Warren denounced the victim. "I think Burdick was murdered, and he got just what he deserved. He should have got it before."

BURDICK

"Got What He Deserved"

Former Husband of Mrs. Helen Warren Gives His Views on the Buffalo Tragedy.

J.B. Warren's bitter comments about Ed made headlines.

Warren said that before they moved to Cleveland, he and his wife spent a lot of time with the Burdicks, the Pennells, and the Paines. They had all gone on a camping trip together a few years earlier.

Asked for his thoughts about Ed Burdick, Warren freely admitted he had disliked and distrusted Burdick from the moment he met him and credited him with causing problems in his marriage. "I told my wife to stay away from him. I told her mother, too," he said emphatically. "That's what started all the trouble."

He was sure his ex-wife had not given Burdick the clipping of the divorce notice. XXXIV

"What do you think about Arthur Pennell?"

"I don't think Pennell killed him. I have my own notion as to whether Pennell had anything to do with the murder or not, but I have not told a living man what my notions are." Warren was, apparently, unwilling to disclose his theories to the press.

"Did Pennell commit suicide?"

"I don't believe Pennell committed suicide," Warren said. "I don't think he had courage enough to end his own life." Warren let out a short, humorless laugh. "Besides, the idea of committing suicide in an automobile is preposterous. Why should he take his wife with him to kill himself?"

Despite Mr. Warren's insinuations, Mrs. Warren and her father said Ed Burdick did not break up her marriage.

The police did not know what to make of the wreck. Certainly, it was possible that it was an accident. The road was quite dangerous, especially with the rain and wind and darkness falling. No guard rail was in place to prevent a sliding car from falling into the quarry. Arthur's words and demeanor in the saloon did not give anyone the impression that he was considering suicide.

An illustration of the flight into the quarry

Yet Arthur was known to be deeply depressed and frightened. And what could account for the Pennells strange behavior during their drive? Why did they remove the top of their auto in the rain?

Carrie Pennell had warned Ed that "Arthur doesn't regard life any too highly." And now all three of them were gone.

Inevitably, questions about money began to emerge in the papers.

The Pennells were known to have a considerable amount of money, but the newspapers revealed they were richer than anyone had realized. Carrie Pennell was a woman of considerable wealth. She had inherited money prior to her marriage, and the year before her death, she inherited another significant sum. Arthur also had inherited money, and he earned a good income as an attorney. He had heavily insured his life. Altogether, the estate was valued at $400,000, which is roughly $12 million dollars in 2020.

Despite the money being accounted for, speculation began to appear in the press about how the Pennells became so wealthy, and wild stories began to appear about how Pennell's wealth might be tied to Ed Burdick's death.

STARTLING STORY, WHICH WILL NOT DOWN, IS THAT PENNELL WAS "COLLECTING AGENCY" FOR CLIQUE OF OFFICIALS WHICH SHOOK DOWN LAWBREAKERS FOR TIDY SUM ANNUALLY

THOUGHT BURDICK MAY HAVE MET DEATH AT PENNELL'S HANDS BECAUSE HE CAME INTO POSSESSION OF PAPERS TELLING OF "DEAL"

The press didn't hesitate to publish wild conspiracies.

On March 13, news broke that Ed Burdick had rewritten his will shortly before his death, cutting his wife out completely. His business partner Charles Parke was named as guardian to his children and trustee of the property he left for them. His estate was valued at $60,000, which is the approximate equivalent of $2 million dollars in 2020. It was to be shared between the three girls equally.

Ed, however, had either forgotten or postponed updating his $25,000 life insurance policy. Half of this sum was for his children, while the other half was divided between his wife and other family members. Alice was still the lawful beneficiary of $10,000 from Ed's life insurance.

She willingly provided a key to her safe deposit box to the police. In it, they found a $50,000 bond from Arthur Pennell, that guaranteed $25,000 to Alice in November 1902. The combined total left her with a substantial sum of money, and her attorney immediately expressed their intention to contest the provision of Ed's will that named Parke as the guardian of the children and their property.

The Inquest Begins

Four days after Arthur Pennell's dramatic death, the inquest into Ed Burdick's death began.

At the turn of the century, inquests in the United States were far more common than they are today. An inquest is an informal investigation conducted by a public prosecutor as to the cause and manner of a suspicious or unusual death. It often shines a light on wrongdoing and may be followed by a criminal trial or civil action. Sometimes the public description of events and the damage to a person's reputation is considered sufficient, and no further action is taken. xxxv

The wheels of justice turned rapidly in 1903. A modern inquest might require months of planning, but the Burdick inquest began 15 days after Ed was murdered. On Saturday, March 14, the courtroom was packed, mostly with women and reporters, and many people had to be turned away.

There was naturally a lot of curiosity about a particularly brutal murder of a well-known local man, but local interest in the inquest was born of something deeper. Victorian social norms and behaviors were commonplace, and they placed heavy emphasis on chastity, purity, and virtuous behavior. These norms were rigidly enforced, and any violation was viewed as an affront to all of society. The erring person could expect to be dealt with severely, typically by being ostracized in some way.

The social code for men was more relaxed and more forgiving. A man whose behavior violated these norms could find that his reputation suffered, but he could demonstrate contrition and eventually be welcomed back into polite society.

This wasn't the case for women. An ostracized woman could never resume the place she once held in society. Alice Burdick, for instance, would never be able to thoroughly reconstruct her reputation after it was ruined when people learned of her affair with Arthur Pennell.

PROSPECT PARK MATERNITY HOSPITAL

ORGANIZED 1900.   INVESTED CAPITAL, $27,000.00

"PROSPECT AVE."	"ELMHURST"
FOR UNMARRIED CLASSES	FOR MARRIED LADIES EXCLUSIVELY
723 PROSPECT AVENUE	CORNER FARGO AVENUE AND
ALL BUSINESS TRANSACTED AT DOWNTOWN OFFICE	CONNECTICUT STREET
58 WEST GENESEE STREET	DR. W. W. TURVER, RESIDENT PHYSICIAN, OWNER
NEXT TO STAR THEATRE	AND SUPT. OF BOTH HOSPITALS, 252 CONN. ST.

An ad in the 1903 Buffalo directory contained a vivid example of the rigid social code, designating different hospitals for "married ladies" and "the unmarried classes."

The wealthier class to which the Burdicks belonged were expected to set the example for the middle and lower classes. Alice, therefore, was doubly guilty. She abandoned her role in society and committed intolerable transgressions. The details of her countersuit had slowly leaked in the press and implicated Ed as well.

Justice Thomas Murphy would preside over the inquest in the police court, and District Attorney Coatsworth was tasked with fulfilling the responsibilities of the state.

News that Gertrude Paine's name was on the witness list swept the town like an electric current. Without a doubt, Mrs. Paine had dominated the headlines in the story of the Burdick murder, and she provided a window into Ed Burdick's personal life and thoughts. However, the press lavished a disproportionate amount of attention on her.

Editors, realizing her image sold papers, kept her in the news far longer than they otherwise would have. In fact, many articles written about Mrs. Paine had little to do with the investigation into Ed's murder.

This photograph of Gertrude Paine, taken on her wedding day, was reprinted in many articles.

"I will never have my picture taken again," she said to one reporter. "How Eddie Burdick got hold of it is more than I can say." XIX

Gertrude insisted she disliked the attention, lamenting that "the newspapers haven't treated me with any sense of decency." This grievance does not ring entirely true, as Mrs. Paine was the only person connected with the case, outside law enforcement, who was giving interviews to the media, and all press descriptions of her overflowed with admiration.

She made the following statement to *The Buffalo Enquirer* before the inquest:

Some of the so-called Elmwood set have said I was a hypnotist. They have tried to connect me with Fred Freeborn's suicide. It is laughable. I wish I could hypnotize some of these reporters who are daily interviewing me in their minds.

As to the report that Edwin Burdick and others were in my power, it is an outrageous and atrocious falsehood, a lie told without the slightest regard for a woman rendered defenseless in the eyes of the public.

The same article provided a detailed recitation of Mrs. Paine's gown and jewelry and offered this description of her person: "Quite an attractive woman in face and figure is Mrs. Paine. Her eyes are of bluish-gray and piercing. She is dramatic in her conversation. Her eyes sparkle with a fire that thrills. She is a woman of remarkable reserve and speaks in a voice filled with emotion. She is clever in her conversation but not especially talkative. Altogether, Mrs. Paine is a woman of remarkable qualities and a winning way." xxxvi

The public would have to wait to hear from Gertrude. The first day's witnesses were Deputy Medical Examiner Dr. John Howland, Detective Sergeant Holmlund, Mrs. Hull, and Maggie Murray.

Dr. Howland was the first witness on the stand. He described receiving a call to come to 101 Ashland Avenue on the morning of February 27. Coatsworth led him through a detailed description of Ed Burdick's wounds. "There were a number of wounds, but the first blow or two would have killed him," the doctor testified.

"Could those wounds be caused by someone being beaten with a .32-caliber Smith & Wesson revolver or a .32-caliber Iver Johnson revolver?" Coatsworth demanded.

Dr. Howland gave a decided negative. xxix

The doctor said that Burdick had died about 2:00 a.m. The DA asked, "Do you think he was moved after he was killed?"

Howland said he was sure the victim had been killed in the den. "But he must have been in some other position when he was killed," Howland said. "There was brain matter and blood on the couch 12 or 15 inches from where the body was resting, and there was no brain matter behind the head. There were bloody fingerprints on the legs, as though someone had pulled him down, and the undershirt had ridden up."

Dr. John Howland, deputy medical examiner

"Was the victim dressed?"

"He was wearing an undershirt. That's all," the doctor replied. The DA asked whether Ed's clothes could have been removed after he died. Dr. Howland shrugged. "No, how could they? They would have been covered with blood, as the undershirt was."

"Could he have been asleep?"

Dr. Howland considered. After a moment, he said, "I can't say. He did have defensive wounds– two fingers on his left hand were broken, as though in an attempt to ward off a blow."

"Did you talk with Dr. Marcy about the victim's cause of death?"

Howland said that Dr. Marcy told him he didn't know whether it was a suicide or a murder when he arrived. "He talked about the divorce scandal and how more scandal would damage the children."

"I asked to see the body. When I saw Burdick's head wounds, I told Marcy it could not possibly be reported as a suicide."

Detective Sergeant Holmlund was the next witness. He was sworn and described the body and the crime scene. "His pants were folded carefully across the foot of the divan," he remembered. "And there was a loaded revolver in his coat pocket."

"Did Dr. Marcy talk to you?"

"Dr. Marcy kept interrupting," Holmlund said with a frown. "He wanted things kept quiet."

When asked about Mrs. Hull, Holmlund shook his head. "I wanted to talk to Mrs. Hull," he said. "But she kept out of my way."

When Detective Holmlund stepped down, Justice Murphy banged the gavel. "We'll recess for 20 minutes." Mrs. Hull would be questioned when the break was over.

Mrs. Hull

Mrs. Hull entered the courtroom, supported on her attorney's arm. She was a small woman clad in a black dress, a dark coat with a sable fur collar, and a black hat with long black plumes. She was sworn and seated. Only then did she lift the heavy white veil that had covered her face, revealing colorless skin and keen blue eyes that darted around the courtroom from behind gold-rimmed glasses.

Mrs. Hull had a square face with sharp features and a firm jaw. Her iron gray hair was pulled back tightly and wound into a bun. Before she began her testimony, she slumped forward and supported her head on one arm, with her fingers partially shielding her face. Only her right eye was visible while she was on the stand, giving her the appearance of an ancient cyclops. Her voice was initially quiet and weak, then Justice Murphy asked her to speak up so all could hear her. The posture of the witness did not change, but gradually her voice had taken on its normal strength and volume.

The witness gave her name and address and said she was 64 years old. Her only child, Alice, married Ed Burdick seventeen years ago. She and her husband had lived with their daughter's family for many years. Mr. Hull died four years earlier, and Mrs. Hull helped care for her grandchildren.

A photograph of Alice with her daughters (L-R) Alice, Marion, and Carol, circa 1899

She said her daughter had been away from home when Ed was murdered. "She wrote two or three times a week, and I wrote to her about as often."

"And you telegraphed. When did you last telegraph, before the telegram you sent to notify your daughter of Mr. Burdick's death?"

"Two or three weeks before Mr. Burdick died." Mrs. Hull said Alice's telegram said she had not received any letters from her mother for a few days and asked if she was ill. Mrs. Hull had responded, "Am not ill."

"Are you sure it wasn't two or three days?"

"I don't think so."

Mrs. Hull testified that she had agreed to show the detectives the telegram but insisted on keeping it herself.

Coatsworth looked at her dubiously. "You say you allowed the officer to see the telegram?"

"I did."

The DA had caught her in a lie but he didn't bother to emphasize the fact. He was apparently satisfied with getting Mrs. Hull on the record. So, instead of pointing out that the police contradicted Mrs. Hull on this point and had never seen the telegram, he merely moved on to the mysterious bottle Ed had brought home. Mrs. Hull said she didn't remember the label, but the bottle was filled with dark liquid. She hadn't seen it since.

"And the bottle is considered missing. Is that right?" When the witness assented, Coatsworth asked, "What do you think became of that bottle, Mrs. Hull?"

The blue eye did not blink. "I haven't the least idea."

Coatsworth asked Mrs. Hull to account for her time from after dinner Thursday night to the point when Ed's body was discovered.

Mrs. Hull replied that she went into her bedroom after putting the children to bed and did not leave it again until 7:30 a.m. She was in the bathroom getting dressed when Maggie called up the stairs to her that the front door and a back window were open. She came downstairs and opened the den door. "I called to him, but he didn't answer. I told Maggie to go to the drug store and call Dr. Marcy."

"You were told the front door and the back window were open, and Mr. Burdick's bedroom was empty. Why did you go look in the den?"

"I don't know."

"You knew that Mr. Burdick might be sick and in need of medical attention. Why didn't you go in there?"

"I could not do it. If he had been sleeping, my screams would have awakened him."

"You screamed?"

"Yes, as loudly as I could. I was afraid to find him dead in there."

"What reason did you have to expect to find him dead in there?"

"None, except he didn't respond to my screams."

"Why did you close the door after you called in to the den?"

"I can't tell," Mrs. Hull said. Her face was expressionless.

Coatsworth walked to his table and rifled through a folder. He pulled out a photo of the crime scene and dropped it in front of Mrs. Hull. "Is this the way the den looked that morning?"

Mrs. Hull barely glanced at it. "It was dark. I could see nothing."

Coatsworth offered a gruesome image of Burdick's body after the quilt and pillows were removed. "What about this one? Is this how the body appeared after Dr. Marcy arrived?" Rather than put the photograph down in front of her, he held it out to Mrs. Hull, requiring her to take it from him.

Her hand shook slightly. "That is Mr. Burdick. Yes, that is how he was found."

Coatsworth took the photographs back and deposited them in his folder. Then he asked, "What did you say when Dr. Marcy came in?"

Initially, Mrs. Hull said she did not remember, but finding Coatsworth would not move on, she said, "I think I said 'I am afraid something has happened.' But I'm not sure."

Coatsworth guided her through her efforts to shield the children from as much of what was happening as possible. Before the doctor arrived, she told Marion her father was sick in the den. After Dr. Marcy told her Ed was murdered, she took the girls upstairs and told them their father was very sick.

"Did you ask Dr. Marcy any questions when he told you Ed Burdick was murdered? Did you ask what happened? How was he killed? Anything like that?"

"No."

"No questions at all about your murdered son-in-law?"

"No," Mrs. Hull repeated. In the experience of the district attorney, most witnesses would have hastened to add some sort of explanation to such a statement. But Mrs. Hull made no attempt to soften this bold statement.

Coatsworth then asked about matters between Burdick and her daughter. The people in the courtroom collectively leaned forward, holding their breath. The cause of the Burdicks' divorce was well known, but no one could guess how the Burdicks handled things between them.

She said Ed told her they were getting divorced the day Alice left. The same day, divorce papers were served.

"Did Mrs. Burdick say anything when she was going?"

"She said she was going to Niagara Falls." Mrs. Hull said she knew why her daughter was leaving; the night before, she witnessed her son-in-law telling her daughter that she had to go.

Coatsworth wanted to know if she had tried to plead her daughter's case. The witness replied that she had not and added, "I supposed he had a right to send her away."

"Oh. You thought he was correct to send her away?"

"No, he had a right to, if he wished to." Mrs. Hull said she asked no questions of her daughter or her son-in-law of the impending divorce. Mr. Burdick, however, confided in her at times.

"Didn't you tell Mr. Burdick that you thought he was as much to blame as she was?"

"No, I didn't think he was as much to blame. My daughter had been very imprudent."

"It's been reported that there was quite a fight at the house there, the weekend before Ed's murder."

"There was not."

Coatsworth lifted an eyebrow. "Your testimony is that you and Burdick were *not* quarreling? You never said anything to him about sending his wife away? Not a word?"

"No."

"There are reports you refused to speak to Mr. Burdick after the divorce papers were served."

"That isn't true."

"Weren't you of the opinion Mr. Burdick was partly to blame for their failed marriage?"

"I think if he had done differently, she would have too."

Coatsworth paused. "In what respect ought he to have done differently?"

"A good many," Mrs. Hull replied. "I cannot think of any way in particular."

Coatsworth eyed Mrs. Hull. She was a remarkable witness. She made few gestures or movements while on the stand and did not expound on her answers unless he demanded specifics. Dressed all in black, with her face in the shadows, a person could be forgiven for thinking she was merely a frail older lady. Coatsworth believed she was nothing of the sort.

It was obvious to Coatsworth that Mrs. Hull was far from devastated by her son-in-law's death. She made no overtly hostile remarks about him, but her demeanor was cold.

Hoping to pierce her armor with an unexpected question, he asked, "You didn't think Edwin Burdick was very broad-minded, did you, Mrs. Hull?"

"No."

"You think he was narrow-minded in a good many things?"

"Yes, a good many things. He *was* narrow-minded." She would not give any examples.

At the inquest into Ed's death, his mother-in-law described him as narrow-minded.

"Your daughter had been sent away before, had she not?"

Mrs. Hull said Alice had left home twice. Ed had moved out once, too.

"Did you send your daughter any money?"

Mrs. Hull denied this. "I began paying rent to them about a year ago, but I sent my daughter no money after she left."

Coatsworth surprisingly did not follow up to ask Mrs. Hull why she started paying rent years after she moved in with the family or whether she continued to pay after Alice left. Instead, he asked why she stayed in the house after her daughter moved out.

"Partly for the children's sake. For Mr. Burdick's sake, too. And love for my daughter."

Coatsworth indicated he was finished with the witness. Mrs. Hull had been on the stand for nearly three hours. She rose and made her way past the court recorder and down the center aisle. The reporters watched her closely, and as the heavy white veil came down over her face, they saw her lips curl into a smile.

Mrs. Hull (highlighted) *emerges, head down, from the courtroom after testifying on the first day of the inquest. The carriage awaits her.*

Maggie Murray was called next. Coatsworth walked her through the morning of the murder and called out the two contradictions between her testimony and that of Mrs. Hull.

Maggie said she went to Mrs. Hull's bedroom to tell her about the open door and window, and Mrs. Hull answered the door fully dressed. The DA demanded, "You're sure it was her *bedroom*?"

"Yes, sir."

"And you say she was completely dressed?"

"Yes."

"Mrs. Hull said she was dressing in the bathroom when you came to speak to her."

"No sir, it was her bedroom. She was already dressed." Maggie could not be budged on this point.

Maggie also said it was her idea to call Dr. Marcy. Once again, when the DA challenged her on this point, Maggie said she was positive.

"Just one more question, Maggie," Coatsworth said. "Do you know who was in the cellar that morning? Was Mrs. Hull down there at all? Or Dr. Marcy?"

Maggie looked confused. "Katie was down there early, and Alfred come over later. They are the only two, to my knowledge."

Court was adjourned until Monday afternoon.

Maggie Murray contradicted details in Mrs. Hull's testimony.

Mrs. Hull's cold testimony and evident lack of feeling for Ed Burdick did not create a favorable impression. "It was remarked Saturday evening that the testimony given by Mrs. Hull tended to show that in the house in which Burdick was killed, his death created little sorrow," *The Buffalo Courier* opined. "It was brought out that when the dead and mangled body of the man was lying in the den, the family appeared more anxious to have breakfast prepared and the furnace attended to than to plan the capture of the assassin." XXXVII

In Defense of Mrs. Hull

Reverend Levi Powers, the minister at Church of the Messiah, spoke to the press Sunday evening. The Burdicks and Mrs. Hull were his long-time parishioners, and he was indignant at the way Mrs. Hull had been treated at the inquest.

He released an angry press statement, aimed at District Attorney Coatsworth. Though he sought to clear Mrs. Hull and put the blame on Arthur Pennell, his statement is most notable for his remarks about Alice. Powers began by saying it was improbable that the real facts of the murder would ever be proven.

> *DA Coatsworth evidently has a theory. He has had it from the first and apparently has it still. I do not know all the facts or supposed facts that cause him to cling so tenaciously to his theory, so I am slow to criticize.*
>
> *All things are possible. Physically, Mrs. Hull could have committed the murder, but I am morally certain she never did. Mrs. Hull was the last person on earth who had a motive to kill Edwin Burdick.*
>
> *Mr. Burdick knew Mrs. Hull was a better mother to the Burdick children than Mrs. Burdick was; that she was more fond of her grandchildren than her own daughter. Burdick frequently said that the children would not miss their mother so long as their grandmother was there.*
>
> *Mr. Burdick was kind to her and spoke of her in the highest terms. He declared the children were better off with the grandmother than with their mother. And Mrs. Hull knew the children were better off with the father than the mother.*
>
> *Mr. Pennell, the one person of sufficient motive, is dead. He was the betrayer of an unusual friendship. He robbed his friend of his wife, ruined her reputation, brought shame to*

the children, and now, by a death skillfully contrived to deceive, leaves the suspicion of murder upon the mother of the woman he wronged. XXXVIII

One of the reporters looked skeptical. "If you suspect Pennell as having something to do with the crime, how do you account for Mr. Burdick being found with only an undershirt on?" he asked.

Reverend Powers pointed at the reporter. "You people have seized on that fact as an indication that a woman was present and killed him. *I* see nothing inconsistent with the theory that Pennell did it. Mr. Burdick may have gone to sleep in the den and Pennell could have obtained the key and suddenly struck him down."

The minister said Burdick told him that he forgave his wife, and he tried to keep his home together. Pennell, he told reporters, led Mrs. Burdick to believe he would obtain a divorce from his wife and marry her while attempting to make his wife believe that he would *not* do this. "He had a strong hypnotic influence over Mrs. Burdick and his wife." XXXVIII

The Inquest Continues

Justice Murphy banged his gavel a few minutes after 2:00 p.m. on Monday March 16, and the court came to order. The only important witness that day was Dr. William Marcy.

Dr. Marcy had been highly embarrassed by Dr. Howland's testimony and had given several interviews over the weekend defending himself.

"I WAS MISQUOTED," SAYS DR. MARCY.

Burdick Family Physician De-clares He Did Not Say Suicide.

The Sunday papers published Dr. Marcy's denials.

With Coatsworth prompting him, Dr. Marcy testified that he had been the first to arrive at the home the morning of the murder, at Mrs. Hull's specific request. He described the disarray in the den and how he had only disturbed the way the quilt was wrapped around the head enough to confirm it was Burdick. Based on the tart, the cocktail, and the body being undressed, he concluded Burdick was killed by a woman visitor. His only other contribution was his fear that listening to the testimony was bad for Mrs. Hull, who had a weak heart.

Dr. Marcy said he told Mrs. Hull that Burdick was dead. "She wrung her hands and asked, 'How can I ever tell the children?' She seemed shocked."

"Was Mrs. Hull crying at this point, Dr. Marcy? Did she ask you what had happened or how it happened?"

"No, but she was depressed and worried." Dr. Marcy said he had proposed a solution regarding the children. "I told her that I would tell the children their father is sick and not likely to recover. Mrs. Hull went upstairs to get them and bring them to the dining room, and I spoke to them there."

Coatsworth raised an eyebrow. "*You* told the children their father was ill?"

"Yes."

Without pointing out that the doctor's statement contradicted that of Mrs. Hull, Coatsworth pivoted to his medical opinion. "Were you of the opinion Burdick was murdered?"

"Not positively."

"How many suicides have you seen where the deceased beat themselves to death and wrapped their heads up in a quilt afterwards?" Coatsworth inquired innocently.

Dr. Marcy flushed a deep red at the sound of suppressed giggles in the courtroom. "I came to agree with Dr. Howland's assessment that Mr. Burdick was murdered."

"But you asked Howland to say it was a suicide, didn't you?"

"No, I didn't!" Dr. Marcy snapped. "After we saw the body, we went to the parlor and I asked, 'Do you think there is a possible suicidal theory? It would save his name and the name of his family.'"

"Save his name, how? Why would suicide be better?" Coatsworth demanded.

"I thought it would have been better for his memory, you understand, if his death was thought to be suicide, if the facts warranted it."

The DA sensed Dr. Marcy's evasiveness and was unwilling to permit it. "No, I do not understand. Why would it be better for his memory?"

Dr. Marcy sighed. "Because of the condition of the room, the fact the body was not dressed, and the talk of divorce proceedings. It looked a little shady at first sight." xxxix

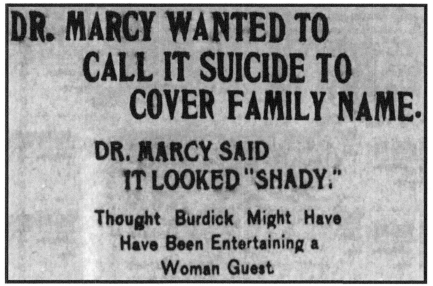

DR. MARCY WANTED TO CALL IT SUICIDE TO COVER FAMILY NAME.

DR. MARCY SAID IT LOOKED "SHADY."

Thought Burdick Might Have Have Been Entertaining a Woman Guest

Dr. Marcy explains his request to Dr. Howland.

"I did not urge Howland to make it a case of suicide. I wanted him to be cautious for the family's sake."

"Do you know what Mrs. Hull was doing while you were talking with Dr. Howland and attending to matters with the body?"

"Well, after I called Howland and Mr. Burdick's friend Parke to come over, she asked me if I wanted breakfast. While I was eating, she came in with a directory and said she needed to send a telegram. I assumed she was notifying her daughter."

The rest of the day was taken up by unimportant witnesses, including cab drivers who had driven fares they did not recognize to the Elmwood Avenue area and a patrolman whose beat was in the vicinity of Elmwood Avenue.

Puzzle Pieces

On Tuesday, March 17, the newspapers published a letter Ed Burdick had written to his mother in January, detailing Pennell's legal maneuverings related to the divorce:

> *"He put in an amended answer to my complaint making counter-charges against me, and asking for custody of the children and alimony.*
>
> *There is no question about the outcome. I shall get my divorce, but I am going to let the matter go slow for a time. I am in no hurry now, and it may be two to six months before it comes to trial.*
>
> *I think he is trying to desert her—to find an excuse for a quarrel—and I am going to give them time to do it. I am not worrying about the matter very much."*

Mrs. Paine arrived Tuesday afternoon to provide her testimony at the inquest. She swept into the packed courtroom with queenly grace and a uniformed officer guided her to the front of the room. She was sworn and perched gracefully on the witness stand.

The court spectators strained to get a good look at Mrs. Paine, while the reporters scribbled descriptions of her velvet coat with white fur collar and turban trimmed with squirrel fur. The dentist's wife did not disappoint those who had read of her as charming and she maintained her composed demeanor throughout her testimony.

"Her voice was that of a woman of a refinement," *The Evening World* wrote approvingly, "her manner that of a well-poised woman of the world. She thoroughly understood the ordeal she was to go through, and was prepared for it. There was a trace of weariness in her tones, betraying the distastefulness of the entire proceeding, but she held herself well in hand, betraying her inward struggle only by a frequent moistening of her lips and a dry cough." [XL]

A sketch of Gertrude Paine testifying at the inquest

Gertrude was likely named in Alice's divorce suit as a corespondent, although little evidence suggests she had an affair with Burdick and even less that she was in any way involved in a murder. She was at the inquest because she was a friend to Ed Burdick, someone in whom he confided, and a friend to the Pennells.

Her testimony was a summary of what she had already told police. In response to the DA's questions, she said she had never heard Mr. Pennell had threatened to harm Mr. Burdick.

"Well, did Mr. Burdick ever threaten to harm Mr. Pennell?"

"Once he said, 'Who would take care of my children if I had a murder on my hands?'" Gertrude remembered. "But he said he would forgive Pennell for all that he had done if he would only marry Mrs. Burdick. He said he would permit her to have the children six months of the year."

"There was a report the Pennells would be divorced. Did Mrs. Pennell ever discuss that possibility with you?"

"Well," Gertrude hesitated. "Mrs. Pennell said she had heard the story but that she had no intention of doing anything of the kind. She said she had spoken to Mr. Burdick about taking his wife back."

Coatsworth said, "You spoke to Mr. Burdick by telephone less than 24 hours before he was brutally murdered. Was there anything strange in what he told you? Or did things seem otherwise amiss?"

"Not at all."

With that, Justice Murphy dismissed Mrs. Paine.

Ed's friend and business partner Charles Parke offered his evidence regarding Burdick's strained relationship with Pennell and what little he knew of the Burdicks' crumbling marriage.

He was eager to defend his friend. "I have never believed a woman committed that murder or got into his house, or that he had any communications with immoral women of any kind."

Without being prompted, Parke stated his belief that Arthur Pennell was behind the murder of his friend, whether he actually killed Ed or not.

"Why do you say that?" Coatsworth asked.

The witness said Ed told him both the Pennells pleaded with him to drop the divorce suit, even after legal action began. "Pennell had been making a further appeal to him and said things which Mr. Burdick understood to be a threat of suicide. I think he said he threatened to kill Mrs. Burdick and himself if that suit were not discontinued. Burdick told me he thought the threat was a bluff."

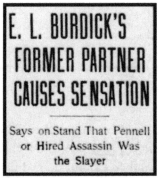

Charles Parke openly accused Arthur Pennell of causing Ed's death.

Coatsworth had a bone to pick with the businessman. "Why would anyone at the house on the morning of the murder *not* wish to aid the police, Mr. Parke?"

Parke immediately became guarded. "I know of no reason why. I don't know that anyone there did not wish to aid the police."

"You don't?" Coatsworth looked pensive. "Then why did you and Dr. Marcy block the immediate investigation, which should follow the discovery of such a terrible murder?"

Parke, discomfited, replied, "Well, after giving the matter due thought, I concluded that both I and Dr. Marcy had acted indiscreetly."

"Of course, had you not intervened as you and Dr. Marcy did perhaps those initial investigations would have turned up something more than they did."

Parke did not speak.

"Why did you repeatedly block the family from being questioned?" Coatsworth insisted. "What was your objection, sir?"

Parke looked alarmed and he stuttered as he answered. "I—I really intended no hindrance to the authorities. I didn't desire to divert suspicions from any guilty person or persons." Charles Parke admitted he tried to block the questioning of Mrs. Hull and the Burdicks because Dr. Marcy suggested they should. "He was in charge when I got there, and he asked me to do it."

"You did not worry that you might be tying things up by suggesting the family required an attorney to be present during questioning?"

Parke said he had no opinion as to whether an attorney needed to be present. "I didn't realize I was tying things up."

Justice Murphy dismissed Parke.

DA Coatsworth next called Alfred Brookman, the elderly man who Ed hired to care for the Burdicks' furnace and keep it in working order.

Alfred said he had seen Mrs. Hull in the cellar the morning of the murder, and she was talking with a gentleman he did not recognize.

"Did you hear any of what they were saying?"

"No. I'm hard of hearing, sir."

Brookman didn't recognize the gentleman, and did not believe he could identify his voice.

Justice Murphy brought down his gavel sharply, causing spectators to jump. "Let's take a short break before the last witness," he said. "Recess for 15 minutes."

Marion Burdick Amazes Everyone

Sixteen-year-old Marion Burdick entered the courtroom with a firm step and looked without interest at the large number of people crowded there waiting for her to speak.

The eldest child of Ed and Alice Burdick raised her right hand and swore to tell the truth. Unlike her grandmother, she did not attempt to hide her face but gazed at DA Coatsworth with a bored expression.

Coatsworth saw at once that she would be a difficult witness. She answered "yes" or "no" as often as possible in response to questions put to her. She never voluntarily elaborated on any answer. When the DA asked her the same question, phrased slightly differently, Marion raised her voice sharply and repeated, "I don't know."

Marion's testimony was that she had eaten dinner with her father, grandmother, and two little sisters then talked to her father for a little while afterward. Later, she went upstairs to her bedroom and went to sleep. Like her sisters and grandmother, she heard nothing during the night. She couldn't—or wouldn't—add anything to what was already known about the day of the murder.

In response to Coatsworth's detailed questions, Marion said her grandmother had told her that her father was very ill in his den. Dr. Marcy had not yet arrived. The witness indicated she had asked no questions about her father's illness.

"When you got up on Friday morning, what did Mrs. Hull tell you?" asked Mr. Coatsworth.

"She said papa was dead."

"Where were you when she told you that?"

"In the dining room."

"She said nothing else to you?"

"Up in my room before that she said he was very ill in the den."

"Was that before Dr. Marcy came?"

"Yes."

"And what did you say?"

Marion replied that she had said nothing. Mrs. Hull didn't volunteer any more information and she hadn't asked.

"Well, what did you do?"

"I went downstairs and left my books in the hall," Marion answered.

"You knew your papa was in his den and that he was very ill and nobody was in there taking care of him?"

"Yes."

"Wasn't he a good papa?"

"He was."

"But you didn't want to go see him?"

"No."

"Well, what *did* you do?"

"I went with Grandma to water the plants in the conservatory," Marion replied calmly.

For once, DA Coatsworth was nearly at a loss for words. Marion's icy calm and reserve seemed inhuman.

"Who told you that your father was dead?"

"Grandma."

"What did Grandma say to you? I mean, how did she tell you?"

"She said, 'He's dead.'"

Coatsworth attempted to frame his question again. "Grandma told you, 'Papa is dead' or—"

"She said, 'He's dead.'"

Marion admitted she had asked nothing about her father's death, including how he died.

DA Coatsworth was genuinely puzzled and demanded, "But why did you take so little interest in your father?"

"I knew that when it was proper for me to know Grandmother Hull would tell me," Marion replied demurely.

Marion Burdick, on the day she testified at the inquest into her father's murder

"And you weren't the least bit curious to know what caused his death?"

"No." The girl's face was as expressionless as her voice.

"Did you ever ask her about his death?"

"I asked later if it was suicide. She said she didn't know."

Coatsworth did not remark on this, but it was an odd answer. Why did Burdick's daughter, like his business partner, make a point of asking whether he had committed suicide? And Mrs. Hull knew for a certainty that Burdick had been murdered at this point. Why would she tell Marion she didn't know if his death was suicide?

Slowly, painfully, the DA pulled from Marion her reaction to learning her father was murdered.

"Did you ask who murdered him?"

"No," the monotone voice replied.

"Didn't you think it was strange that your papa should be found murdered in his own house?"

"Yes."

Coatsworth asked whether Marion had any idea who had murdered her father. When she said she had not, he asked, "Haven't you given any thought as to who might have done it?"

"Yes."

"And what was your conclusion?"

"I don't have one."

Coatsworth moved on to her parents' impending divorce. Marion said her father had explained everything to her.

The DA tried to be delicate. "From what you understood of the trouble between your parents, can you say that you were– well, in sympathy with your father?"

"Not altogether," Marion replied.

"You did not altogether sympathize with your papa in regard to the stand he had taken with your mother."

With a barely perceptible shrug, Marion replied, "I sympathized with him."

In response to the DA's next questions, the girl said she loved her father, and he was kind to her.

"And you thought he was right?"

"I don't know."

Coatsworth questioned her briefly on what she had said to her mother about Arthur Pennell, but the girl maintained she had never broached the subject with her mother.

Marion's cold, emotionless answers were jarring to the DA, Justice Murphy, and members of the press who were observing the proceedings. Reporters covering the inquest wrote, "When describing the awful scene in her home when her father's mutilated body was found, Marion appeared as unconcerned as though she was reciting a lesson at school and manifested perhaps not half as much emotion." [XII]

Mr. Hartzell, the Burdick family attorney, thought he should intervene to help Marion and to redirect suspicion away from Mrs. Hull, where the DA seemed determined to place it. He stood and asked if he might ask the witness some questions.

Coatsworth all but sighed with relief as he sat down. Marion's lack of feeling about the brutal murder of her father disturbed him greatly.

Hartzell sought to soften the harsh exterior Marion had presented. "Papa and Grandma were very friendly, weren't they?"

"Always."

"Grandma loved you? And you loved her?"

"Yes."

Hartzell, it seemed, could ask nicer questions, but Marion was no more helpful to her attorney than she was to the DA.

Coatsworth leaped to his feet. "You and Grandma have talked considerable about this matter since your father's death, haven't you?"

"Not considerable."

"You've talked some about it?" Coatsworth pressed.

"Some."

Neither Coatsworth or Hartzell had any more questions for the witness. Justice Murphy adjourned the court.

Marion's answers and demeanor did not strike anyone favorably, but it's difficult to know how much significance to attach to it. The only other glimpse we have into Marion's behavior is from the newspaper article six months earlier, when she calmly steered her father's burning automobile through the crowded streets of Buffalo. Back then, the newspapers admired her coolness. [1] After her testimony at the inquest, they complained she was an iceberg. [XII]

MARION BURDICK'S STRANGE TESTIMONY WAS LIKE A PIECE OF COLD MARBLE

Marion's testimony was not well received.

Many reports mentioned how similar her behavior was to that of Mrs. Hull, a comparison that all understood to reflect poorly on Marion and her grandmother. The local paper summed it up neatly, if not chronologically: "[Marion] was told her father was dangerously ill in his den, she did not ask whether anyone was with him, whether he needed assistance, or whether she could go to him. When she was told he was dead, she went to the conservatory to water the plants while breakfast was being prepared." XXXVIII

Coatsworth had brought out a key difference between the testimony of Mrs. Hull and her granddaughter. "They differed in their statements regarding the breaking of the news of Burdick's death. Mrs. Hull contended Dr. Marcy had told Marion and the other children of their father's fate and that this was fully an hour after the discovery of the crime has been made. This Marion denied, and said her grandmother first told her of it and that it was before the doctor arrived. This went to approve the claim of the district attorney who had contended all along that Mrs. Hull hated Burdick and knew of his fate before she sent for the doctor." XL

On Friday, the newspapers reported on the gathering cloud of suspicion. "It is worthy of note that while many have directed suspicion at Pennell since his death, the police, who would be expected to do it first, have drawn away from him. They do not believe he murdered Mr. Burdick, although they admit that possibly he was in some way connected with the crime. The police now have another suspect—Mrs. Hull." XLI

The inquest was supposed to resume the following day, but DA Coatsworth came down with a sore throat. When court did return to session, Alice Burdick, the woman who was so intricately tied to every part of the case, would speak out.

Alice, At Last

When court was gaveled back into session, it was immediately evident that interest in the case had not flagged. "The same throng of morbid sightseers congregated about the entrances and struggled for a glimpse of those engaged in the proceedings," *The Buffalo Review* reported. XLII

Coatsworth's sore throat had abated, and he was eager to wrap up the case. He briefly quizzed Burdick's attorney, but George C. Miller could provide no new information about his client's troubles with Arthur Pennell. "When I asked Mr. Burdick about the revolver he was carrying, he said he felt safer with it. He never said Pennell had threatened him."

"When was the last time you saw Burdick?"

"He stopped by my office Thursday in the late afternoon before he went home."

"Did he mention anything about having an appointment with anyone at his home later?"

"No, he didn't," Miller said. "He was in every way like himself."

Coatsworth called to the stand Henry Orrett, the man who tended the Pennells' furnace. He testified that he saw Mr. Pennell about 9:30 a.m., about 90 minutes after Ed Burdick's body was found. He was surprised Mr. Pennell had put coal into the furnace himself.

"He had not done that before?"

"No." Orrett replied.

"Was his demeanor unusual or stressed in any way?"

"No," Orrett said. "Mr. Pennell greeted me just the same way he always did, 'Good morning, Henry.'"

Lizzie Romance was called next. She was sworn and took her seat. Coatsworth wanted only one piece of information from her. "Did you see the Pennells on Thursday, February 26, or Friday, February 27?"

"Yes, sir," Lizzie replied. "I saw them in their bedroom around ten o'clock Thursday night." She confirmed Arthur and Carrie were acting normally. The next morning, they rose at their usual time. She did not hear them get up during the night.

The witness was dismissed.

Had his life not been cut short so violently, Alice would have ceased to be Ed Burdick's wife two weeks earlier. Instead, she entered the courtroom in deep mourning, closely veiled, the picture of a grieving widow. She was flanked by Mrs. Hull, Mr. Hartzell, and another attorney, Mr. Hubble.

The newspapers described her admiringly. "Just a little woman is Mrs. Burdick. When at school, she was known as Sweet Alice. Remarkably petite and full of life, Alice Hull as a school girl and as a society woman was a general favorite with all who knew her. She is perhaps 35 years old, weighs 100 pounds, and is less than five feet in height … Mrs. Burdick has very large black eyes. Her nose is not quite straight and her mouth is just a trifle large. In dress, she is a model of perfection." [XV]

Coatsworth guided Alice through an introduction. She described herself as the 42-year-old widow of Ed Burdick and mother of three.

Alice Burdick takes the stand.

She met Arthur Pennell about five years ago at a card party. She had gone to New Haven with the Pennells to watch the 1898 commencement at Carrie Pennell's especial request.

There was no unusual friendship between her and Mr. Pennell prior to the trip, she told the DA. When he asked what happened between them at New Haven, Alice replied, "Nothing of importance."

Coatsworth approached the stand with a package of letters in his hand. "Do you recall receiving a letter from Mr. Pennell in September of 1900, written from New Haven?"

"No, sir."

"I'll read it," the DA said. "'Yesterday, I was at the gateway on the Campus Grounds where more than two years ago, I drew you in the darkness. This place is enshrined to me.' Now do you remember receiving it?"

Mr. Hartzell jumped to his feet. "May I ask what the purpose of the DA's question is?"

It was a natural objection for Alice's defense attorney to make. No direct tie had been established between Ed's death and Alice's affair with Arthur Pennell, so the question could be considered irrelevant.

Justice Murphy said encouragingly, "You can object to her answering any questions that might hold her up to public ridicule."

"We trust that no unnecessary questions that would hold the witness up to public ridicule will be asked," Hartzell replied serenely, reseating himself. He said not another word throughout Alice's testimony, which by most standards seemed designed to subject her to public ridicule.

Coatsworth turned back to Mrs. Burdick and held up the letter. "You don't remember this?"

The witness indicated she now recalled the letter Coatsworth had quoted.

"You recall it now. Did you object to his conduct?" Alice replied that she thought she had, but couldn't remember. She admitted she had not told her husband or Mrs. Pennell of the incident.

The DA pulled out the letter in which Pennell described finding Alice's gloves and read it aloud. Mrs. Burdick did not recall it, but conceded it was addressed to her in Pennell's handwriting.

"What does 'I will meet you at 1-2-3 on Wednesday' mean?"

"I don't know."

"What does he mean by 'the paradise within your arms?'"

"I don't know."

"What did he mean by 'fate is inexorable unless we choose to break it?'"

"I've no idea."

"'I have had your dear picture in the locket to look at, and that has been awfully sweet and a great comfort.' Did you give Mr. Pennell a locket with your picture?"

"Pennell got the locket and had the picture made from a larger photograph."

"Pennell got the locket," Coatsworth repeated. A reporter in the courtroom was watching the DA and thought the scene he was witnessing was extraordinary. "DA Coatsworth was coldly impassive. The more merciless the question, the less emotion he displayed in asking it. There was evidently no sympathy in his heart for Pennell nor for the unabashed woman who sat before him so calmly and unblushingly relating the stories of her sinning." [XII]

"He referred to you as 'my love, my life, dearest one'?"

"I don't know."

The DA smiled. "Are you sure, Mrs. Burdick, that you don't know?"

"I'm as sure of that as I am of sitting here," she replied.

"It *is* addressed to you?" Coatsworth waved the envelope at Alice. She acknowledged it was. "And you do not remember it?"

"No." It was a peculiar thing, but Alice Burdick, who had claimed to love Arthur Pennell with all of her being, could scarcely remember anything about him ten days after his death.

"It is Arthur Pennell's handwriting, and it is addressed to you, isn't it?"

"Seems to be."

"Now," DA Coatsworth pronounced. "I will read this letter to you and see if it won't refresh your recollection." Alice stared at him, as bored as though she were watching a play she had seen dozens of times.

District Attorney Edward Coatsworth

As I looked into your beautiful eyes last night I feared that there was some trouble hidden there that I did not know. I was not sure but I was afraid there might be something more than the fact I was going away. If there was, please tell me, dearest. I cannot bear that you would be unhappy over anything, especially when I am away from you. At one time I thought that it might be owing to some difference with your husband. When I think of how he has treated you, I feel I must kill Ed Burdick!"

The DA paused impressively.

But I hold my temper, knowing that an expression of even a small part of my feelings would probably lead to a quick and

> *violent quarrel, which would make matters harder for us*
> *both.*

Even the beautiful poetic writing could not withstand Coatsworth's strident delivery. It was just the type of circumstance Arthur had dreaded and seems to have been specially constituted by the district attorney to humiliate Alice and vilify his memory.

Alice said she didn't recall it, despite having listened to Coatsworth's dramatic reading of one of the passages.

Coatsworth thrust the pages at her. "Read it, and see if it helps you recall."

Alice took her time, reading through each page. When she was finished, she put the papers down.

"Well, Mrs. Burdick?"

"I don't remember it."

Coatsworth snatched up the letter and waved it at Justice Murphy. "Your Honor, this letter was found in Ed Burdick's pocket the morning of the murder," he said.

For more than two hours, Coatsworth quizzed Alice on every line of every letter, but found her memory to be uniformly poor.

At last, Justice Murphy announced a brief recess.

When she was back on the stand, Alice was confronted about the fight on New Year's Day 1901 between her and Ed regarding Pennell's letters. Alice said Mr. Burdick had become aware of her close friendship with Mr. Pennell that day, but added that her husband continued to throw them together afterwards. With this implausible claim, Alice seemed to be implying that Ed bore most of the responsibility for the affair with Arthur.

Under the DA's persistent questioning, Alice revealed that her husband asked her what she had done the previous afternoon, and she admitted she had been out walking with Mr. Pennell. "He told me I'd been very imprudent, and it was a foolish thing to do, which I know."

It was not, she admitted, the first time she'd gone walking with Mr. Pennell, but it might have been the first time Ed had found out about it.

"Do you remember taking this box here—" DA Coatsworth held Alice's tin box aloft, "and giving some letters to your husband?"

"No," Alice said. "I remember I *opened* the box." There was suddenly an edge in her voice.

"Were these letters in the box?" Alice's memory failed her yet again. It was a long time ago, and she thought some letters might have been in the box, but she could not remember who they were from or what they contained. "I forgot about it, and Mr. Burdick never told me."

"Why did you open the box?" Coatsworth asked.

"He forced me to." Alice said Ed grabbed her by the throat and compelled her to open the box. He then took the box and the letters away.

"Why was he so anxious to see what was in the box?"

"I don't know," Alice said. She couldn't remember any conversation she and Ed had ever had about the letters, nor could she recall that her husband ever confronted her about Arthur.

Later, her mother informed her that Ed had given her the box for safe-keeping, and asked Alice what had happened.

The tin box was never returned, but Alice soon rented a safe deposit box. It wasn't her idea, she explained. Mr. Pennell asked her to do it. "He wanted me to keep valuable papers in it, detective papers on Mr. Burdick."

"You employed a detective to gather evidence because you were anxious to get a divorce?"

"I didn't employ him," Alice said. "Mr. Pennell hired him and paid for him."

"Why were you anxious to be divorced from your husband?" the DA demanded.

"I had no love for him," Alice replied. Her tone was so matter-of-fact that even Justice Murphy looked at her in surprise. When Coatsworth did not ask another question, she added, "We'd grown apart. I thought we would be happier. And I loved Mr. Pennell."

"You didn't have any love for Ed Burdick?"

"I had respect for him," Alice replied.

"You say you loved Mr. Pennell. You were aware that there was already a Mrs. Pennell?" Alice said nonchalantly that Arthur wanted a divorce. "What did Mrs. Pennell say about that?"

"Sometimes she said she would, sometimes she would not." Alice had never spoken to Mrs. Pennell about it.

"Why did your husband order you to leave in May 1901?" the district attorney asked.

"Why, he thought I was—had been imprudent with Mr. Pennell and told me I must go." She had left Buffalo, she admitted, leaving her children with Ed and Mrs. Hull.

"How long were you away before you began to write to Mr. Burdick, begging him to take you back?"

When Alice did not know, Coatsworth obligingly produced a letter from Mrs. Burdick to her husband and that was dated May 22. The letter was several pages, and the DA read every word to the court. "That was a begging, beseeching letter, wasn't it?"

"Yes, sir."

"Mr. Burdick wanted Mr. Pennell to leave Buffalo permanently before he would allow you to come home, didn't he?"

"Yes, but *I* couldn't compel him to go."

Alice Burdick

"You promised if he let you come back, you would be a good girl?"

"Yes, and I made that promise in good faith," Alice replied.

"And did you keep that promise, Mrs. Burdick?"

"I'm afraid I didn't."

Coatsworth held up another letter. "In this passage, your husband makes mention that you have replaced your lawful wedding ring with one from Mr. Pennell."

"It wasn't a wedding ring."

"But you wore it instead of your wedding ring that your husband gave you?"

Alice looked at him coolly. "There was no significance to that."

A note of incredulity crept into the DA's voice. "And you say your husband was willing take you back, after all this, even after you had been doing wrong?"

"He didn't believe I had been doing anything more than being imprudent. He told me so."

The DA pointed out that when Alice returned to Buffalo three weeks later, Mr. Pennell was still in town. After she came home, she admitted to meeting with him regularly.

"After all these promises that you wouldn't?" Coatsworth questioned, feigning mild surprise.

"Only because Mr. Pennell constantly solicited me to do so," Alice stated. He had continually contacted her and pleaded to see her. They met by appointment in the parks, in street cars, and at the library. "But it was always in the morning or early in the afternoon," Alice insisted.

By a long series of yes-or-no questions, Coatsworth established Alice had also met Pennell at both of his offices and at least five private addresses in town. "Do you remember a room Mr. Pennell rented on Seventh Street? A furnished apartment?"

Alice reluctantly acknowledged she had been there once or twice. Mr. Pennell always arrived first and let her in.

"It was furnished, wasn't it?" Coatsworth asked innocently.

"Yes," was the guarded reply.

"Do you remember the day when you were there with Mr. Pennell and Mr. Burdick came there with two detectives to confront you and Pennell?"

"Yes."

"You were there, in that apartment, but somehow you managed to leave without Mr. Burdick seeing you. How did you get out?"

"I didn't know it was Mr. Burdick at the door," she replied calmly. "I thought it was some stranger, and I left the room through the window."

"Where did you go?"

Alice folded her hands. "I went to church." Justice Murphy permitted the crowd in the courtroom to laugh.

Though she admitted Ed told her that evening she must leave, Alice insisted that he did not hold her responsible. "He said he did not blame me as much as Pennell. He said Pennell was more to blame than I was."

Justice Murphy banged his gavel. Court was adjourned for the day.

Alice Burdick returned to court the next day. Overnight, the press had become disenchanted with her. She had not made a favorable impression the day before and uncharitable descriptions of her had appeared in many of the newspapers.

"Mrs. Burdick was frank in the extreme," one report read. "She rehearsed many things that would have disturbed most women, but her eyes never moistened. Mrs. Burdick is anything but good-looking, having a long nose, puffed cheeks, low forehead, and retreating chin." [XLIII]

The aim of the district attorney was clear to court-watchers. Coatsworth's interrogation of Alice was an attempt to show that the death of Burdick was due to a conspiracy, and Arthur Pennell was the man with a strong motive to be the arch-conspirator. [XII]

When Mrs. Burdick returned to the stand, Coatsworth pounced. He asked if she had physically attacked Ed the day he had forced her to open the tin box. When Alice denied it, he asked, "Wasn't it necessary for him to wear a piece of plaster on his head and ear after you struck him over the head with a chair?" Alice denied this.

A sketch of Alice at the inquest

Coatsworth asked her about Ed's stay at the Genesee Hotel in January 1902 and revealed to the court that around that time, Ed Burdick was again threatening to divorce his wife. He read aloud the letters between Ed and Alice.

"When Mr. Burdick announced his intent to secure a divorce, you said you were crushed and that Mr. Pennell's leaving Buffalo was only delayed temporarily," Coatsworth declared. "Did Burdick come home after he received this letter?"

Mrs. Burdick said she had gone to his office to plead with him and at last, Ed relented and returned to their house. Nothing more was said of divorce.

"But it was right after this that you had those clandestine meetings with Pennell, wasn't it?" Coatsworth asked skeptically.

Instead of replying directly, Alice gave a familiar answer, "Mr. Pennell continually besought me. And my husband threw us together constantly."

Coatsworth moved on to December. "When your husband ordered you to leave in December of last year, you went to Niagara Falls. Who was with you?"

"Pennell."

After a few days at Niagara Falls, they traveled to New York City, and Alice registered at the Hotel Roland. Alice acknowledged she saw Mr. Pennell daily when he returned to the city with his wife, and Carrie knew she was in the city.

"Why didn't you see Carrie?" Coatsworth asked. "Weren't you friendly with her?"

"Not particularly." Alice wasn't aware Mrs. Pennell had been writing to Ed during that week.

Coatsworth read Carrie's letter to Ed aloud. "What do you think she meant by 'you know his romantic nature, how it would appeal to him to go and take her with him?'"

"I've no idea," Alice replied.

"Here's another letter she wrote a week later." Coatsworth read Carrie's last letter to Ed, begging him to take his wife back as an act of charity for his children. Alice, however, exhibited no interest in Mrs. Pennell's letters.

She admitted Ed had offered her partial custody of their daughters when she met him at the Genesee Hotel in January. They had discussed the divorce. "I told him then that it was Pennell's fault the divorce proceedings were slowed."

"Then you did *not* plan to contest his suit? You were willing for the divorce to occur?" the DA demanded.

"At the time I was," Alice responded. "But afterwards, I thought I would make a defense and save my honor."

"You weren't going to contest the divorce when you thought Mrs. Pennell would agree to a divorce from her husband?"

"That's right. Later she said she wouldn't."

Coatsworth demanded, "So it wasn't until Mrs. Pennell refused to divorce her husband that you decided to launch a countersuit against Burdick?"

Alice hastened to distance herself from any responsibility. "*I* didn't. Pennell decided everything."

The DA was curious. "And what did Mr. Pennell plan to do after you were divorced?"

"He said he would go out west and get a divorce and marry me." Alice said she believed he was sincere.

The DA looked at her curiously. "But even after you launched the countersuit, you wrote to Mr. Burdick, pleading to be allowed to come home."

He read Alice's letter to Ed aloud. "If you believed Mr. Pennell would marry you, why did you want your husband to take you back?"

Alice was silent.

"Mr. Burdick feared you only wanted to come home until the Pennells divorced, then you would leave him to marry Pennell. Was that what you wanted to do?"

Still the witness refused to speak.

Coatsworth had his answer. He moved on. Alice said she took her keys with her when she left home in December. "You made duplicate keys while you were in New York City, didn't you?"

Alice denied this and swore Pennell never had a key to her home.

"Why did you send a telegram to your mother two days before Mr. Burdick's murder?" he demanded. Alice explained that her mother usually wrote two or three times a week. When she did not receive a letter in five days, she became worried. Her mother replied that she was well.

When Coatsworth asked to see the telegrams, Alice said she didn't have them. "My custom is to destroy my letters."

"What an odd custom. Why do you destroy them?"

"I don't care to have the maids rifling through my letters and personal affairs," the witness sniffed.

"When you came home, after learning Mr. Burdick was dead, did your mother tell you any details about the murder? Did you ask her for more information?"

"No," Alice said.

"Did Mrs. Hull know of your relations with Pennell?"

The subject had never come up between them until she returned home after Mr. Burdick's murder. When pressed by the DA, she admitted, "She knew I was very friendly with Mr. Pennell. She blamed me for being imprudent."

Coatsworth rifled through some papers and produced a copy of a bond. "Pennell purchased this bond for you, leaving you $25,000."

"I don't know anything about it."

"Now, how could that be, Mrs. Burdick?" the DA asked irritably. "The bond was in your safe deposit box." Alice maintained she had never seen it, and had not known of its existence.

Coatsworth signaled he was finished with the witness.

Attorney Hartzell rose. "When Mr. Pennell found out that your husband had seen his letters to you, he was agitated, wasn't he? He felt he had been disgraced."

Alice admitted Arthur was a sensitive man and was distraught when he learned Ed had seen his letters.

"You didn't give or lend him a key to your home, did you?"

"Certainly not. I do not believe Arthur Pennell would have murdered Ed."

"In your letters to your husband, you promised to be a good girl if he will let you come home. When you returned, did you resist Pennell and refuse to meet him?"

"I did." Alice explained that though she had acted in good faith, she was helpless against Mr. Pennell, who constantly waylaid her and pleaded with her to meet him. For a long time, she refused to yield to his infatuation with her. Even when she did, though, there was nothing really wrong between them. "Arthur's conduct toward me at all times was that becoming of a gentleman to a lady. He was a man of high moral character, and the accusations against him are outrageous."

A sketch of Justice Murphy questioning Alice Burdick

Suddenly, Justice Murphy spoke. "Did not you know that Mrs. Pennell loved her husband? Didn't she feel that you had wronged her?"

"I don't think so," Alice shrugged. "She knew it was Arthur's fault."

Coatsworth stared at her. "Maybe she did love her husband, and that's why she did not agree to a divorce."

The witness responded acidly. "She only dreaded the publicity and the scandal."

Mr. Hartzell cleared his throat. "Mr. Burdick and Mrs. Pennell were very friendly?"

"Yes," Mrs. Burdick said. "Mrs. Pennell had been to our home many times. She was quite familiar with the den."

"Could a person tap on the window of the front door and attract the attention of anyone in the den without ringing the bell?" It would be easy to do, Alice acknowledged.

"Did anyone tell you Mrs. Pennell was at Mr. Burdick's home on the night of the murder?"

"No, sir."

The witness was excused. Alice Burdick stood and covered her face with a long mourning veil, obscuring her features. Without a backward glance, she hurried from the courtroom.

Though Coatsworth's reading of every line of each letter was tiresome, he had nevertheless acted as an emissary of justice. Through him, the voices of the dead had confronted Alice Burdick, and her duplicity was laid bare to the world.

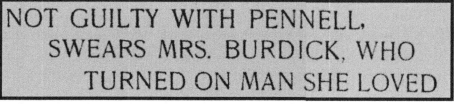

NOT GUILTY WITH PENNELL, SWEARS MRS. BURDICK, WHO TURNED ON MAN SHE LOVED

When questioned about her actions, Alice continually shifted the blame to Arthur Pennell, even as she claimed to love him.

Over the course of three days of testimony, Alice had managed to dispel the press's early admiration and replace it with a decided distaste. Reporters criticized her emotionless responses and transparently false claims to have forgotten important events and conversations. The press was particularly offended by Alice's evident lack of feeling and eagerness to blame Arthur for her actions. "The long-nosed shifty-eyed woman in black on the stand heard all those letters read without a qualm." [XLIV]

Despite her suspected dishonesty, Alice had nevertheless provided valuable insight into the case. *The Buffalo Enquirer* opined that there was serious doubt Pennell was guilty of the murder. His letters revealed him to be a romantic, sentimental man. His unscrupulous behavior had wrecked Burdick's home, the paper conceded, but no evidence pointed to Pennell as the killer, or even indicated that he would be capable of murder.

Most importantly, Alice's testimony offered a glimpse into Ed Burdick's character. "[Burdick] was a solitary individual, pitted single-handed against a merciless array of antagonistic events and hostile personalities, which were closing in on him with irresistible force.

"His wife was lost to him. His home was ruined. His close friend had betrayed him … The stricken man was brave and noble. Time after time, he consented to forgive and forget. But the force of fate was too powerful … His life was blotted out in the swift agony of a violent death." [XLV]

Thirteen-year-old Carol and ten-year-old Alice followed their mother to the stand. Like their mother, grandmother, and older sister, they displayed little emotion.

Carol described sitting on her father's knee with her sister, Alice, on his other knee. "He used to read to us or play games with us in the evening."

"What else did he do that evening?" the DA asked.

Carol thought for a minute and said, "He shined his shoes in the bathroom." He had come in later and kissed them good night. Carol said that sometimes Marion slept in Mrs. Hull's room, but she had not slept there the night of the murder.

"When you woke up Friday morning, where did you first see Grandma?" the DA asked.

Carol said her grandmother was in the hall, already fully dressed.

"That is all, little one," Justice Murphy intervened. "Step down."

Little Alice was the last witness of the day. Of all the children, the wide-eyed little girl was said to bear the greatest physical resemblance to her father.

"I knew Papa was sick," she said. "As soon as I got up, Grandma told me."

"Didn't you want to go see him?"

"Yes, but Grandma wouldn't let me."

"Did you know where he was?"

"Yes, in the den, lying on the sofa."

"You knew that before breakfast?"

"Yes. Grandma said somebody had come in during the night and hurt Papa."

When pressed, however, the child grew confused and said she thought she learned her father was sick after breakfast.

"Few sadder scenes have been seen in any courtroom," *The Buffalo Review* pronounced. "The mother giving testimony concerning the death of her husband and her relations with the man for whom she had been unfaithful. This followed by her little children … both of them all through their lives to bear the mark and the memory of that courtroom, the image of the eager faces of the vulgar crowd and to feel the fright of strange surroundings." XLII

The Last Witnesses

On the last day of testimony, before the courtroom even opened its doors, the morning headlines reported the findings of the automobile experts who examined the Pennells' electric carriage. They unanimously declared Arthur Pennell tried to avoid the accident. It was certainly *not* a suicide, they said. Mr. Babcock, the mechanic who tended to Pennell's auto, heartily agreed and added the machine was in top working order.

In the courtroom, Carol Burdick, Ed and Alice's second daughter, was recalled. After confirming her grandmother slept alone on the night of the murder, the girl revealed that on the morning of the murder, she and her little sister, Alice, overheard Katie Koenig and Maggie Murray discussing the open door and finding Mr. Burdick had not slept in his room. She remembered her little sister had said, "I heard Papa go downstairs a while ago."

It was clear she was not referring to Maggie Murray, who had descended the stairs only a minute or two before she ran back up. According to police reports, Maggie was thought to be the first person downstairs that morning.

Little Alice was not recalled. She had forgotten many of the details of the day of the murder already, and it was unlikely she could provide reliable testimony on this point.

If this testimony was accurate, then someone in the house walked downstairs ten to twenty minutes before the cook descended from the third floor.

The DA seemed to be insinuating that Mrs. Hull went downstairs for the purpose of creating the impression a burglar had been in the house. If true, it was incriminating evidence of her involvement in Ed's murder. However, the testimony was unsubstantiated and came from a 10-year-old child. It might be considered a possibility, but it was too flimsy to be decisive.

As expected, Mrs. Hull was recalled. She was again dressed all in black but this time she sat up straight in her chair and her voice was strong.

Coatsworth first pointed out the discrepancy between her testimony and that of Maggie Murray, who claimed she had gone to Mrs. Hull's bedroom to notify her of the open door and window. The cook testified that Mrs. Hull was fully dressed. Mrs. Hull denied this and repeated her story of dressing in the bathroom when she heard Maggie calling to her.

Coatsworth did not linger. He wanted to question Mrs. Hull about Arthur Pennell. "How well did you know him?"

"Not at all," she snapped. "I did not like him."

"You say you've had no interactions with him?"

Mrs. Hull acknowledged she had written to Mr. Pennell in January 1901. "It was a very earnest letter," Mrs. Hull said. Her eyes twitched behind her glasses. "I thought he was going to make trouble in the family. I appealed to his pride."

"And did Mr. Pennell reply?"

"He did not." Mrs. Hull shut her mouth tightly. Two years had passed since she had written to Arthur and he was no longer living, but Mrs. Hull was still incensed when she recalled this snub.

"That surprised you?"

"If he had any heart and soul, it would have appealed to him, I am sure," the witness replied. Coatsworth did not ask whether Ed or Alice knew of her interference.

"Was it the only time you wrote?"

"I wrote once more in May and asked him to leave the city. He replied in a very cold manner, and said he would not be driven out of Buffalo. He said there was a better way."

"Did you ever see Mr. Pennell again?"

"Once. He was in his automobile."

"He acknowledged you?"

"He tried to raise his hat, but I turned my head."

Mrs. Hull was dismissed.

The third witness was the Reverend Levi Powers.

"I counseled Ed about his marital difficulties, twice," he testified. The first time, the reverend had gone to Buffalo Envelope Co.

"At whose request?" Coatsworth demanded.

No one had asked him to go, Reverend Powers answered. He had heard rumors and decided to call on Burdick.

"No one asked you. Did you ever talk to Mrs. Hull about it?"

"Yes," Powers confessed reluctantly. He had spoken to Mrs. Hull about it three days before he called on Burdick.

The reverend quoted her as saying, "Allie is not without fault, but if you knew the whole thing, you would not think the fault is all on one side. Burdick will get his divorce, and I don't see why Mrs. Burdick and Mr. Pennell should wish to fight it."

Mrs. Hull did not ask him to do anything, Powers hastened to explain. He had gone to see Burdick and talked to him for an hour. Ed told him that if Pennell and Alice did not drop the countersuit, he would have Pennell's letters to Alice published. "He said it would make Mr. Pennell look ridiculous."

"I urged him to take his wife back, but he gave me the impression he wouldn't do it."

"Did he ever mention Mrs. Hull?"

"Oh, I think he felt very kindly toward her. She wasn't well, and Burdick had offered to send her to California or Florida, but the doctor said she was better off at home with the children."

The next witness was the city chemist. He had analyzed the contents of Burdick's stomach, and found a small amount of alcohol. "He drank a cocktail, or part of a cocktail, sometime after dinner." The contents showed no poison nor any traces of the crackers, cheese, and tart found in the den.

The final witness was Detective Malcolm Cornish. Detective Cornish had stayed largely in the background of the case, and he was not on the stand long. Much of the framing of the case in the press relied on the circumstances in which Ed Burdick's body was found in his den, particularly that he couldn't have been wearing clothes, except for the undershirt. The clean clothes at the base of the sofa were pointed out as evidence Burdick wasn't wearing them at the time he was murdered. The police did not inform the press when they discovered the blood stains on the drawers, but the detective now testified to it.

Cornish produced the bloody undershirt Burdick had been wearing when he was killed. The brown wool was covered with thick black stains. He produced the victim's underwear, which was clean. "You see here," Cornish said, pointing to the waist. "There is a stain here." He turned them over and held up the right leg. "There's another small stain here, which I believe to be a fingerprint."

Cornish said he believed the victim was disabled after one blow to the head. "Then the murderer seized the underdrawers with bloody hands and drew them off."

Coatsworth reminded the court that a bloody fingerprint was found on Burdick's leg as well, and that the body had been pulled down about 12" or 15" from the head of the sofa.

Cornish's other evidence was that the glass found on the tray in the den had a sticky surface. "It was as if the liquor had been spilled over its entire outside."

Justice Murphy closed the inquest, saying he would announce his findings the following day.

The press paid little attention to the last day of testimony, and limited their coverage of the inquest to a paragraph or two. The public had lost interest in the proceedings after seeing Mrs. Paine and listening to Arthur Pennell's love letters. To those who were more knowledgeable about the case, it was one of the most interesting days.

Another Surprise

Though Justice Murphy intended to share his conclusions Friday, the court did not reconvene until Monday. When it did, it was not to listen to the justice's findings. A surprise development caused District Attorney Coatsworth to send a request to Justice Murphy, asking him to take the surprising step of reopening the inquest.

The Buffalo Police Department buzzed. For two weeks, Chief Cusack quietly sat beside Justice Murphy slowly putting the final pieces of his criminal jigsaw puzzle together. Now, at this critical moment, when the picture was imperfect but unmistakable, it was about to be upended.

Two new witnesses had come forward. DA Coatsworth had received a letter, written in a fine hand, from an insurance salesman named Alexander Quinn. In the letter, Quinn explained he had been following the Burdick case in the newspapers and he recognized photos of Arthur Pennell and Alice Burdick. He had seen the couple in early December, when he was working as a bartender at Hotel Roland.

"I got to know Pennell quite well during his stay at the Roland," the letter read. "One day when he was somewhat intoxicated and in a talkative mood he said to me, 'There is one man in this world I'm going to kill even if I go to the gallows for it.'"

Coatsworth was inclined to be suspicious, in part because the Hotel Roland billed itself as temperance lodging. He gave the letter to Chief Cusack, who wired the New York City police department. A detective was dispatched to investigate and found a second witness named F.J. King, a cashier from the hotel's buffet. King corroborated Quinn's story, saying he had overheard the conversation with Pennell. The detective told Coatsworth he thought the witnesses were credible, and the DA immediately subpoenaed both men. [XLVI]

The press rushed to New York City, clamoring for a detailed statement, but local police ordered Quinn and King not to talk. The press would not have to wait long. The men would be in Buffalo to testify Monday, March 30.

When the men appeared in court, the press was immediately wary of the two. "Looking more like a clergyman and businessman than an insurance solicitor and bartender, Messrs. King and Quinn gave their testimony." [XII]

Alexander Quinn took the stand first. "Pennell came into the barroom on the evening in question," he testified. He said Arthur asked for the railroad timetable and had several drinks with the bartender. "Pennell gave me his personal card and told me I ought to have a better job than that of a bartender, and I told him I should be glad to have a better job if he could get it for me," Quinn testified.

According to Quinn, Mr. King joined them as Arthur offered his critique of some French photographs on the wall. "After several more drinks, Pennell said, 'You boys don't know what is passing through my mind tonight. There's one man I could kill if I have to go to gallows for it! At the same time, I am having the best time of my life at another man's expense.' The next morning, Pennell entered the barroom at about eleven o'clock, and we exchanged toasts."

King corroborated Quinn's account. "He said there was one man he could kill even if he had to swing on the gallows for it. We had drinks—he, Quinn, and I—and I proposed a toast to our new friend. Pennell responded with a toast to death. I can't remember just how it went. 'Here's to Death!' that was one thing he said."

Both men identified a photograph of Arthur Pennell as the man to whom they were referring.

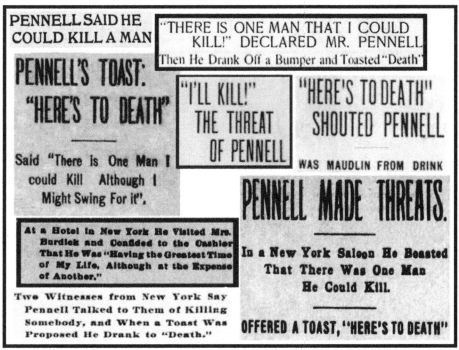

A selection of melodramatic headlines following testimony from the surprise witnesses

The press, though delighted with the sensationalist headlines the two had provided, considered Quinn and King to be far from credible. They were increasingly skeptical of how much of the guilt was being cast upon Arthur Pennell, with minimal evidence.

Reporters were almost incredulous when they discovered the DA and the police appeared to be taking these last-minute witnesses seriously.

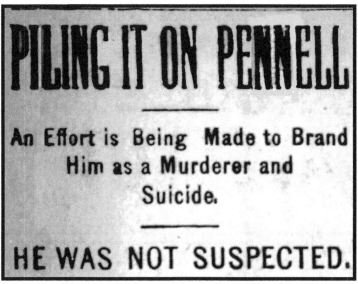

Headlines hinted at reporters' skepticism of Pennell's guilt

The police and the DA regarded the two witnesses very differently, and believed the testimony of Quinn and King to be credible and definitive. Though the DA seemed to have been wavering on the identity of Ed's murderer and implied that Mrs. Hull was at least indirectly involved, he had put his suspicions aside.

Coatsworth believed the information Quinn and King provided effectively sealed the case against Arthur Pennell.

Justice Murphy's Conclusions

Wednesday, April 1, 1903, was a cold, rainy day. Inside the courthouse, Justice Murphy cleared his throat before reading his verdict.

Justice Murphy

Edwin Burdick came to his death through several blows delivered by a dull-edged weapon, delivered with homicidal intent, Justice Murphy began.

Although the murderer was no stranger, he said, it was not a woman. A woman could not have wielded the forceful blows that killed Ed Burdick. And, he added, "Expert testimony offered that nothing of an impure nature had taken place in the den preceding Mr. Burdick's death."

"At the time of the murder the deceased was living with his three little girls, with their grandmother, his mother-in-law, at their home on Ashland Avenue," the justice said. "His wife, the children's mother, had not been home since the early days of December. For reasons which appear later, she spent the night of the murder in Atlantic City."

The justice outlined the evening before the murder, ending with Margaret Murray seeing Ed downstairs when she came in that night. He described the state of the house as it was discovered the next morning by Miss Murray, with the window and the door standing open. He referenced the testimony that little Alice said she heard Papa go downstairs a little while ago—before Miss Murray went downstairs.

Mrs. Hull testified she was in the bathroom getting dressed when the alarm was raised that the door and window were open. But Miss Murray's testimony was that she spoke to Mrs. Hull upstairs, and she was already up and dressed. Mrs. Hull said she couldn't see anything when she stood in the doorway of the den, but she feared Ed was lying in there dead.

"Someone," Justice Murphy said, "contrived to make the crime scene look like the work of burglars, but the lack of footprints, and the snow and ice on the ledge tell otherwise. No burglar waited in the den to wrap the head of his victim in that blanket and put pillows on his corpse. And, nothing has been missed from the house except Mr. Burdick's gold pocket watch."

Dr. Marcy had advocated for the death to be listed as a suicide to save Burdick's name and save the family a great deal of scandal. He commended Dr. Howland for refusing to accept Dr. Marcy's urging to describe the crime as a suicide. "But for his rugged honesty," the judge said. "We would not have known that one of the most clever and shocking murders of this or any age was committed at our very doors." This was an interesting and undeniable point. Had Dr. Howland agreed to list Ed's death as a suicide, he would have been buried two days later with no one any the wiser.

"The actions of Mrs. Hull on that morning and her testimony on the stand have caused me much thought and study," Justice Murphy declared. "To my mind, they are inconsistent with a perfect want of knowledge as to what actually occurred. So little apparent feeling for the dead man, such an evident desire to cover up the crime, and no disposition whatever to aid the authorities in apprehending the murderer may be explainable, but they have not been explained."

After a pause, Justice Murphy spoke of the affair between Alice and Arthur. He noted that Mr. Burdick had sent detectives to shadow Mrs. Burdick and Mr. Pennell, and Mr. Pennell had sent detectives to trail Mr. Burdick. But only Mr. Burdick's detectives had been successful in gathering evidence.

MYSTERY DEEPENS

Burdick Inquest Fixes Guilt Upon No One.

MOTIVES ARE PLENTY

Mrs. Burdick and Pennell Had Most to Dread.

LIKE APPLES OF SODOM

Their Love Turned to Dead Sea Fruit.

The judge was preoccupied by the relationship between Alice and Arthur.

Justice Murphy continued to focus on Arthur Pennell. "Where is the motive for this crime?" he asked.

Justice Murphy ticked off the evidence against Arthur. He was the lover of the victim's wife. "She loved Pennell, and he apparently became infatuated with her. His letters to Mrs. Burdick were of such a gushing, love-sick, importuning nature that their publication meant complete humiliation and social ruin to their author."

Justice Murphy spoke of Arthur Pennell's letter to Alice, in which he threatened to kill Ed Burdick and noted that Arthur purchased two revolvers in three weeks. He pointed out Carrie Pennell wrote a warning letter to Burdick.

"And now we have a cashier and a bartender of a New York hotel who have testified that Pennell said he would kill a certain man, even if he went to the gallows for it."

Pennell knew the interior of the Burdick home, and it would be easy to obtain a key. He was with Mrs. Burdick just two days before the murder, and he was in Buffalo that night.

"These facts would, in my opinion, constitute just grounds on which a warrant could be issued, if Mr. Pennell were alive. That would not mean, however, that he is guilty. He would have the right to a trial. But he can never be placed on trial. To the dead there must be given the same justice as to the living. He is innocent until proven guilty."

Finally, Justice Murphy came to Alice. "Marriage is the cornerstone of society," he said severely. "It is something sacredly regarded by all. To make little of it is to forfeit the good will and respect of our people and to invite their most severe censure.

"Therefore, it is our duty to censure Mrs. Burdick. But great as her wrong has been, great is her punishment."

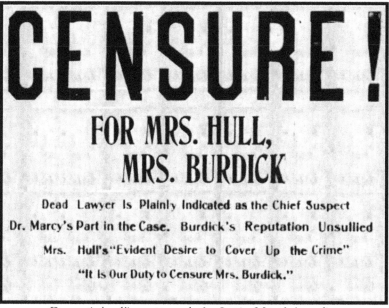

CENSURE!

FOR MRS. HULL, MRS. BURDICK

Dead Lawyer Is Plainly Indicated as the Chief Suspect

Dr. Marcy's Part in the Case. Burdick's Reputation Unsullied

Mrs. Hull's "Evident Desire to Cover Up the Crime"

"It Is Our Duty to Censure Mrs. Burdick."

Dramatic headlines appeared after Justice Murphy's verdict.

Before closing the inquest, Justice Murphy once again underlined his first point. "This inquest has not disclosed a single immoral act on Edwin Burdick's part. Everything portrays him as a loving father and a more than magnanimous and forgiving husband."

And with that, the inquest was closed. Edwin Burdick's murder remains unsolved. No one was ever charged or punished.

Aftermath

Reporters were waiting outside when Chief Cusack left the courtroom, and he gave them a quick, informal statement. "If the facts that have been learned in the last two weeks had been known two days after the Burdick murder, Arthur Pennell would never have had the opportunity to go for that fatal automobile ride. He would have been arrested." [XLVII]

In an interview later that day, the judge elaborated on his ruling. "Mrs. Hull has not told all she knows. I am convinced that she cares little if the murderer of her son-in-law is ever apprehended. If she and Mrs. Burdick told the police everything they knew to be true the very first day, we would have had some one—I don't care to say who—behind bars."

The evening papers delivered a new piece of information that added to the dissatisfaction many people felt with the inquest. Arthur Pennell's attorneys revealed that they had been prevented from testifying at the Burdick inquest or offering evidence which they claimed would disprove many of the accusations.

"Perhaps it was natural that Pennell, the dead man, should have had no one there to take his part," *The Buffalo Commercial* mused. "Yet if a live man is entitled to the presumption of innocence until proven guilty, it seems as though a dead man should not even be accused until all doubt as to his guilt has been removed.

"It will be remembered that during the closing hours of the Burdick inquest, fire from all quarters of the courtroom was centered on Pennell. The district attorney was after him pitilessly. Attorneys Hartzell and Hubble assailed him. Mrs. Hull turned on him with her last breath of evidence. And Mrs. Burdick eagerly, cheerfully, lightly damned him, though she had been a partner in his sin and folly." [XLVIII]

But the voices of protest were drowned out by those who were exuberant over the court's findings.

Coatsworth said the findings were exactly what the testimony ought to have produced. Mr. Hartzell, the Burdicks' attorney who had been living with the family said, "We are well-pleased with the results of the inquest. We do not wish to make any comments on Judge Murphy's findings."

Mr. Hartzell, however, was unwilling to let the negative perceptions of Mrs. Hull, Mrs. Burdick, and Marion go unchallenged. "A good deal of importance has been attached to the apparent lack of feeling by members of the household over Mr. Burdick's death," he said.

It wasn't true, he assured the reporters. "I have been in a position to know of the deep sorrow expressed by them, of the tears that have been shed. I know Mrs. Hull is entirely innocent of this terrible crime, and she had no knowledge of the person or persons who did the deed, and I believe the world will gradually reach that determination. Mrs. Burdick has been wronged, too. She too has been greatly misjudged."

In early April, Justice Murphy presided over the Pennell inquest. It lasted only a few hours, and the justice concluded it was impossible to tell whether the wreck that killed the Pennells was accidental or by design. The court took no further action.

A few days later, Alice gave a remarkable interview to *The Baltimore Sun*. The reporter interviewed her at her home on Ashland Avenue. Over five weeks had passed since Ed Burdick had been struck down so viciously in his den.

"The murdered man's widow, a trim little figure in black, came tripping down the wide stairway into the reception hall. There is something sprightly in her step which makes it easy to believe she was the most graceful dancer in the Elmwood Club," he wrote. "The settled expression of sadness which her face had worn in the courtroom was lacking, and there was alertness in her snappy black eyes."

On the key points, she was consistent with her testimony at the inquest. She stated that she believed an outsider had killed Ed, and indicated she believed he had been entertaining a woman on the night of his murder. Alice said she had tried and failed to think who might have killed Ed. "I should be more anxious to know than anyone else," she told the reporter. "I have heard that suspicion was directed to Mr. Pennell, but I cannot believe he would commit an act like that. There was nothing brutal in his disposition. He was sensitive, high-strung, and emotional and sometimes showed temper when he was angry, but there was nothing vicious in his nature."

As to her relationship with Arthur, Alice continued to maintain it was all perfectly innocent. It was true that she met him frequently after Ed allowed her to return home in the summer of 1901, but her intentions had been honorable. Arthur continually fabricated reasons to see her, such as talking over detective reports. Alice would meet him in good faith only to learn there was no business to talk over.

Alice Hull Burdick, circa 1902

Alice was surprisingly fixated on one aspect of the crime: the food found in the den. "Of one thing I am sure," Alice told him. "And that is that Mr. Burdick did not put that food out for himself. He was dyspeptic and was careful about what he ate. At night, he always ate a little cereal with milk before retiring. He always ate it standing up in the butler's pantry. It's ridiculous to think of his eating cheese or tarts in his den. He would drink to be sociable, so we always had liquor in the house, but it did not agree with him, and he would never drink alone." xii

As the reporter was leaving, he stole a glance at the closed door of the den. A heavy rug was rolled up and laid across the door-sill. Alice noticed and offered, "Do you want to look in there?"

The reporter was surprised, but immediately agreed. Alice urged him to go in, and but she did not follow him.

Nothing could have prepared the reporter for what he found when he entered the room. He wrote of the experience in an article published the following day. "The den has never been cleaned up since the murder. The blood-stained couch is what first attracts attention. Beside the couch lay the blood-stained sofa pillows which had helped to cover the body. Beneath the desk in another corner of the room were a lot of snap-shot photographs which had been spilled by the murderer when he ransacked the drawers. Burdick's gold-bowed glasses still lay on the bookcase where he had left them." xlix

The turn of the century was a time of wonder and optimism. Every day, a seeming impossibility became a reality. Had he lived just ten months longer, Ed would have seen the day when men could fly. Given his studious interest in life around him and his eagerness to be among the first people to drive and own an automobile, Ed would probably have been one of the first people to envision the possibilities of aviation.

Ed had been killed in a brutal attack in his den, but the lives of the family he left behind continued placidly in the house on Ashland Avenue.

Within thirty-six hours of Ed Burdick's murder, Alice moved back in to the home on Ashland Avenue to live with her mother and daughters. She continued to fight for control over the children and Ed's estate in court. Later in the year, she was awarded temporary full custody of her daughters and became the custodian of the property they inherited from their father, despite Ed's explicit directions in the will.

In July, *The Crowley Post-Signal* published a short article updating readers about the Burdicks. Their lives had resumed almost as if they had never been violently disrupted five months earlier. The family was still in Buffalo and continued to occupy the Ashland Avenue home where Mr. Burdick was murdered.

"Almost any fine afternoon, Mrs. Burdick can be seen in the shopping district accompanied by her daughter Marion, the eldest of the Burdick children. Attired in a fashionable summer gown of white, with her pretty daughter, also dressed in light colors, Mrs. Burdick was the most scrutinized woman in the shopping district on two afternoons of the present week."

"The den in which the brutal deed was committed has been thoroughly transformed," the article reported. The couch where Mr. Burdick was murdered, the rugs, pillows, and other furnishings were replaced. "In fact, the den is closed now and is but rarely visited by any members of the family." [L]

The following year, Seth and Gertrude Paine separated in the early fall. Mrs. Paine took a course in stenography and obtained a job to support herself and her daughter. Dr. Seth Paine died suddenly of heart failure in December of 1904. [LI]

In the years following the murder, little is known of the family and what became of them. It's difficult to believe how quickly Alice, her children, and Mrs. Hull faded into obscurity, given the flood of media attention surrounding the murder and the inquest.

Court records show Alice continued to battle in court for money due to her and control over the children's inheritance. The Pennell estate paid her more than $32,000 in 1905 for the bond Arthur had given her, but she was defeated two years later in the appellate courts when she attempted to gain control of Ed's estate.

In February of 1909, Marion married H. Arthur Brereton at age 21. The wedding took place at the bride's home. The young couple moved to Cleveland, and nine months later, their daughter, Marion Alice Brereton, was born. Two years later, Marion died suddenly of peritonitis. She was 23 years old.

Carol married Clifford Weiss in 1915. By then, the Burdicks had moved into a smaller home on Bird Avenue. Alice's fortunes appeared to have declined in her later years. This was the first of many moves, always into slightly less grand accommodations. Eventually, she moved in with Carol's family.

Mrs. Hull passed away at age 85 in August 1923. Two months later, Carol gave birth to her only child, a son she named Donald. The same month, Ed and Alice's youngest daughter, Alice, married Charles Sill, a World War One Navy veteran. The two had a daughter named Suzanne in 1928.

Tragedy again visited the family in the mid-1930s, striking Alice Sill especially hard. Her only child Suzanne died at age 6, in 1934. Then one evening in 1936, Carol died at home. She was 46 years old, and her death was completely unexpected. After Carol's death, Alice Burdick moved to a nearby boarding house close to Elmwood Avenue.

The following year, Charles Sill died of a heart attack in a Buffalo hotel room at age 52. It's difficult to imagine how devastated Alice Sill must have been, having lost her child, sister, and husband in such rapid succession. She eventually moved into the same boarding house as her mother and obtained a job as a private secretary.

The boarding house where Alice lived until her death in 1944.

Alice Hull Burdick passed away in 1944, at age 83. She survived everyone connected with the tragedy of Ed's death, as well as two of her three children, and one of her grandchildren.

If she knew anything that could help bring Ed's murderer to justice, she never told a soul.

A Cold Heart

This book has recorded all the known facts and the conclusions of law enforcement. What follows are the author's views.

Justice Murphy believed that because the circumstances of the murder were public, Ed's name must be cleared and his reputation redeemed. After announcing how the victim had come to his death, the first point the judge made was that "nothing of an impure nature" had taken place in the den before the murder. As he closed the inquest, his last statement reiterated that Ed was a moral man.

The judge summarily dismissed all of the evidence and testimony that suggested a woman committed the murder, stating that women weren't strong enough to deliver the blows that had crushed Ed's skull. It's a dubious claim that the police and medical evidence call into question. The murder weapon was a 2-pound golf putter. The crime scene evidence showed the murderer had taken Ed by surprise, striking as his back was turned. The extensive damage to Ed's head was due, in part, to an unusually thin skull.

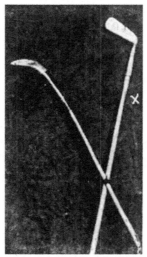

A police photo of Ed's putter and another club was reprinted in the newspaper. The story notes that the putter, marked with an x, has a heavy steel tip.

Though he did not believe the murderer was female, Justice Murphy made it clear the women were not without fault. It was peculiar that neither Alice nor Mrs. Hull displayed any grief about Ed's untimely death; it was strange that they had not been particularly cooperative during the police investigation. Justice Murphy said he believed Mrs. Hull knew more about the murder than she was willing to say, and that she didn't care if the murderer was ever caught. Despite this incredible statement, the inquest resulted in no recommendation to charge Alice or Mrs. Hull as conspirators or accessories to the crime.

The judge next upbraided Dr. Marcy for blocking the police from interviewing Mrs. Hull and for his attempt to falsify Ed's cause of death as a suicide. Dr. Marcy's actions on the morning of the murder are at the heart of the mystery surrounding Ed's death. He was the family doctor and the first to be notified that something was wrong at the Burdick home. Dr. Marcy found Ed's lifeless body and examined his crushed skull.

The detectives became frustrated by the doctor's repeated interference when they attempted to question the occupants of the house after the murder was discovered. Mrs. Hull was Dr. Marcy's patient and he insisted her health was too frail to withstand an interview. Alice's mother was only 64 years old when Ed was killed, and some newspaper accounts note she appeared to be in good health at the time. Reverend Powers also referred to Mrs. Hull being in poor health but was quoted in an interview saying she was physically capable of committing the murder. Even if Dr. Marcy genuinely believed that an interview would put Mrs. Hull's health at risk, his interference that morning went far beyond thwarting the detectives' efforts to question her.

Rather than assist the police in ensuring Ed's killer was brought to justice, the doctor attempted to cover up the murder of his patient. He attempted to prevent a criminal investigation from taking place and endangered his reputation to misrepresent Ed's death as a suicide. Later, he endured public humiliation when his actions came to light.

The doctor never offered a satisfactory explanation for his actions in the hours following the murder. On the witness stand, Dr. Marcy explained that he acted as he did out of a desire to protect Ed's reputation since the scene in the den looked shady. This is not a plausible explanation.

No one asked Dr. Marcy or Mrs. Hull whether they were in the cellar on the morning of the murder, and Alfred Brookman's testimony was not even mentioned in the inquest findings. Yet the doctor's attempts to stop the investigation must have been a reaction to whatever Mrs. Hull had said to him.

Justice Murphy, however, was satisfied with scolding the doctor for interfering without questioning his reasons for doing so. Having ruled out a female murderer, the judge now fixed his attention on Arthur, the lone remaining suspect.

Justice Murphy laid out the case against Arthur Pennell. He had been heard to threaten Ed's life and could have easily obtained a key to the Burdick home. He knew the place well, and his alibi could only be attested to by his wife. Pennell had purchased two revolvers in three weeks, and the witnesses from Hotel Roland swore a drunken Arthur told them he wanted to kill one person so badly, he didn't care if he was hanged for it.

Pennell's motives, the judge said, were his infatuation with Alice Burdick and his desperation to stop Ed Burdick from publishing the letters and disgracing him. And when the police appeared to be closing in on the murderer, Arthur Pennell drove his car off a cliff into the Jammerthal rock quarry, killing himself and his wife. Though he was unwilling to definitively declare Arthur Pennell guilty of the crime, Justice Murphy made it clear that he was confident the deceased attorney was involved in the murder.

It was a surprisingly weak case.

Even with significant pieces missing from the puzzle, the emerging portrait of the killer the police investigation was assembling did not appear to justify Justice Murphy's conclusion of Arthur's probable guilt. Many critical questions went unasked, and numerous gaps and contradictions passed unremarked. The court refused to allow Arthur's attorneys to testify.

Why would Arthur kill Ed, even as he continued to plead with him to take Alice back? He wanted to prevent his letters from being published, but he knew that he had only to drop the counter charges alleging Ed was unfaithful, and the letters would remain private.

The police were initially baffled by what they soon realized was a staged crime scene. At a glance, it looked as though Ed was with a woman and she had killed him. It would not make sense for Arthur to stage the scene this way. As an attorney, he would have been well aware that once Ed died, the divorce proceedings were moot. It was no longer legally relevant if another woman was in his life. Even if he had attempted to stage the scene to compromise Ed, it's doubtful he would have taken the time to assemble a plate of crackers and cheese, a tart, and a small bottle of liquor, knowing every second he remained in the house put him in more danger.

It's also difficult to imagine someone as careful and detail-oriented as Arthur would stage the crime scene in such a confused way. The killer attempted to create the impression of a burglary *and* a murderous female visitor, and the police quickly realized the scene had been staged. Arthur was clever. Had he been wicked enough to kill his former friend and stage the scene, he would have realized the police would be more apt to believe a set of manufactured clues that pointed in a single direction.

There was little physical or circumstantial evidence linking Pennell to the crime. Arthur denied he murdered Ed, and the police believed him. The fact he purchased two revolvers in three weeks' time was unusual. However, even if Arthur had purchased 10 revolvers, it would not shed any light on who beat Ed to death with his golf club. At most, buying the revolvers might be an indication of a suicidal ideation on Arthur's part.

Those who knew him contended Arthur had a withdrawn, dreamy disposition, and was very sensitive about what others thought of him. The nervousness he experienced in the days following the murder could have stemmed from his consciousness of others' suspicions. Not one friend or acquaintance of Arthur Pennell believed he was capable of murder. When Charles Parke warned his friend that Pennell might murder him, Ed rejected the idea at once, saying Pennell was a coward. This is particularly relevant since Ed did fear for his life and in the months leading up to the murder, he carried a revolver with him everywhere.

In the eyes of the law, it did not matter whether Arthur's strange death was deliberate or an accident. It was formally declared an accident by the police, the medical examiner, and a number of experts who examined the scene. The young boys who witnessed the accident said Arthur's hat flew off and he made a grab for it, which could have caused the automobile to veer off the slippery road and into the quarry.

Given Arthur's deep depression and the Pennells' strange behavior in the hours leading up to the accident, it is at least possible that the crash was deliberate. Even if he deliberately drove off a cliff into the rock quarry, it is not convincing proof that he was involved in Ed's murder. Arthur was a wistful, melancholy person. His wife long suspected he was suicidal, and even his letters to Alice frequently seemed sorrowful. It is interesting that after Ed Burdick was murdered, Arthur never saw Alice again.

Justice Murphy had an agenda. He was offended by Alice and Arthur's conduct, and he was eager to make a statement about morality. He wanted to condemn their illicit relationship by linking it to deadly consequences.

That seems to be the only explanation for why he was willing to accept the testimony of the surprise witnesses, Quinn and King, at the end of the inquest as credible. The press certainly didn't accept the men as credible witnesses. Arthur's character, as described by his family and friends, bears no resemblance to the man described by these witnesses, and there is no proof such an encounter took place. Arthur was known to be exceedingly careful about his image, and one can scarcely imagine him drinking with two strangers, while making incriminating statements and raising an absurd toast to death. Quinn contacted the DA only after the story became a nationwide sensation, which calls into question whether these unexpected witnesses may have been more interested in notoriety than justice.

Justice Murphy's fixation on Arthur and evident unwillingness to consider a woman as the suspect probably relieved Mrs. Hull, for she had the same means to commit the murder as Arthur Pennell, with far more opportunities, and a much stronger motive.

Mrs. Hull was never treated as a serious suspect, despite her tense relationship with Ed and her suspicious behavior following his murder. In part, this was because investigators did not think she was physically strong enough to commit the murder, and dismissed the idea that a grandmother from a good family could have committed such a violent act.

However, Mrs. Hull was physically capable of lifting a two-pound putter. The force of a blow would depend mostly on how fast it was brought down. An object brought down with some velocity could strike a murderous blow without requiring much strength. Even a light blow would have incapacitated Ed because of his abnormally thin skull.

At the inquest, DA Coatsworth only lightly challenged Mrs. Hull, even though much of her testimony was contradicted by other witnesses. Mrs. Hull said she had offered to show detectives the telegram Alice sent to her before the murder. This contradicted police records and testimony. Her account of her actions and whereabouts on the morning of the murder were contradicted by several witnesses, but no explanation was given for the discrepancies.

The DA took care to mention how strange it was that, after being notified of potential burglars and that Ed was nowhere to be found, Mrs. Hull headed straight to the den. She called for him but she would not go in, fearing she would find him lying murdered on the sofa. It was a specific and accurate guess but one that did not trouble the court much.

One reason many people did not consider Mrs. Hull to be a serious suspect was that Ed had always spoken so highly of her. He told friends he was grateful to her for staying with the family after Alice went away to Atlantic City. Ed was one of the most prosperous men in Buffalo, and he was known to be generous with his mother-in-law, who was entirely dependent on him.

Mrs. Hull made it a point to tell the court she had started paying rent to Ed and Alice. It's too bad the DA did not ask her more about this. It would be interesting to know where she was getting the money and why she felt it necessary to begin paying rent, after living with the family for many years. It's highly unlikely that he would have asked Mrs. Hull to pay rent, or even been willing to accept money from her.

If Ed Burdick was kind to his mother-in-law and provided for her, why would she murder him? Undoubtedly, his relationship with her had soured after he filed for divorce. According to Detective Boland, the investigator who had been trailing Alice and Arthur, Ed talked to him about Mrs. Hull and said she had seemed to support him at first, but eventually she sided with her daughter. Police were unable to confirm the rumors that Mrs. Hull refused to speak to Ed after he had ordered Alice out of their home in December 1902.

Every aspect of Mrs. Hull's life had been disrupted and threatened by Alice's affair with Arthur Pennell. She acknowledged her daughter bore some responsibility. She said frankly that she disliked Arthur.

Nevertheless, most of her wrath was focused on her son-in-law. She didn't attempt to disguise it, even as she testified at the inquest into his murder. When she was questioned about Ed's relationship with Alice, Mrs. Hull criticized him and testified that he was "narrow-minded in a great many things" and implied her son-in-law could have saved his marriage, had he been more reasonable. Reverend Powers reluctantly admitted Mrs. Hull had minimized her daughter's part in the Burdick's marital woes and implied Ed was more at fault.

It's likely that some of her anger was a result of being manipulated by Alice, who misrepresented situations frequently to avoid any responsibility for them. On New Year's Day 1901, after Ed took away the box of letters, she told Mrs.

Hull that "Ed took me by the throat." DA Coatsworth implied that Alice had been the attacker that day and had injured Ed. We don't know whether Ed seized Alice's throat in the middle of an argument. There is no doubt, however, that Alice told her mother that he had. Such a circumstance would surely inflame Mrs. Hull against Ed, and she probably never forgot it.

Remaining in Buffalo after her daughter's departure was probably not an act of charity on her part. She probably wanted to stay with her grandchildren, but even if she wanted to leave, she did not have the means to live anywhere else. Her only real option was to go to Atlantic City with Alice. With Arthur Pennell's frequent visits, this might have been even more uncomfortable than staying in Buffalo.

No matter how angry Mrs. Hull was about Ed's treatment of Alice, it paled in comparison to the deep fear she must have felt. When Ed finally determined he would move forward with the divorce, he jeopardized her fundamental sense of security. Separations were temporary, but a divorce would permanently change her life.

She could not go on living in Ed's home on Ashland Avenue after his marriage to Alice was dissolved. He was likely to remarry soon—in fact, he was rumored to be seriously interested in the newly-divorced Mrs. Warren. He would begin seeing other women, and eventually another woman would marry him and move into the home on Ashland Avenue. No second wife would appreciate the first mother-in-law's presence. To Mrs. Hull, her place in the home would become more precarious with every passing day.

The specter of Ed with a new woman—a woman who would be eager to cast her out—must always have loomed large in Mrs. Hull's imagination. What was she to do after the divorce? Where could she go? She would have to move in to a dingy boarding house in a cheap part of town or in a cramped hotel room with Alice. In either instance, her luxurious life would be a thing of the past.

Mrs. Hull's behavior after Ed's murder startled everyone. She felt no grief for him. According to her granddaughter Marion's sworn testimony, Mrs. Hull notified the children of their father's death by simply saying, "He's dead." Before Dr. Marcy came over, she refused to go in the den to check on Ed, and ordered the cook to serve breakfast first and then walk to the store to call the doctor and ask him to come to the house.

After Dr. Marcy told her Ed was murdered, she sent a telegram to Alice notifying her of Ed's death, and asked the doctor to call Ed's business partner.

Yet she waited over 30 hours to tell Ed's mother and sister of his death, ensuring they would be unable to attend the funeral. The following day, she and Alice displayed no grief at the interment. All of this bespeaks a deep animosity toward her son-in-law.

She had the motive, means, and opportunity, but that doesn't mean Mrs. Hull was the murderer. However, there was important evidence at the crime scene that further implicates her, including potentially significant aspects details that were ignored or overlooked.

The victim was found in his den, with his body covered by pillows and his head wrapped in a log cabin quilt. Modern forensic science tells us that if a killer covers a victim's face after murdering them, it's often a sign that he or she knew the victim well.

This is supported by the fact that Ed's golf putter was wiped down after it was used to murder him. The murderer knew the body would be discovered within hours, and it would be obvious at once that Ed had been beaten to death. The most obvious reason to clean the golf putter would be to conceal the fact that the murder weapon belonged to the victim. If a stranger or a visitor had come there to murder Ed, it is unlikely he or she would arrived without a weapon to accomplish their goal.

When Dr. Marcy said the crime scene looked shady, he was referring to the fact that Ed's body was found clad only an undershirt. There was a tray of snacks and a bottle of liquor near the divan, but it was obviously for someone other than the victim, who was known to avoid the food it contained and drank only socially.

The tray of food and Ed's missing clothing contributed to the impression that the victim had been killed during a liaison with some unknown woman. Maggie said she saw Ed in his den, clad in his underwear, about 10:15 p.m. the night before. It might have been his habit to read that way, or he might have removed his outer clothing so he could put coal in the furnace without getting his clothes dirty. However, he was undoubtedly wearing drawers when he was murdered, because the murderer's bloody hands had carefully pulled them off after at least one blow had been struck.

The idea of Ed Burdick entertaining a mysterious woman in his den very late at night was improbable to his friends. However, it was just the type of scenario that Mrs. Hull feared. It would not be surprising if she staged the scene to subconsciously mirror a deep fear she felt.

It would also have the benefit of softening the public perception of Alice, by illustrating that it was *Ed* who was carrying on an illicit relationship. By sending his wife away as he twice did, Ed made a statement that Alice's behavior was so intolerable that he refused to stand for it.

In Mrs. Hull's opinion, Ed had exposed Alice to the world's scorn and derision. He had robbed the children of their mother, Mrs. Hull of her daughter, and Alice of her rightful place in society. Admittedly, Alice's behavior was a source of continual embarrassment to Mrs. Hull, but Ed's reaction to it was far worse.

After beating Ed to death, the murderer undoubtedly spent quite a while in the house. The police speculated that anything related to the divorce, including the detective's notes and Arthur's letters to Alice, had been taken by the killer.

If Arthur committed the murder and then searched the den for evidence of the affair to destroy, it seems odd that he would neglect to look in Ed's wallet for additional information. The police found the revolver and the wallet near Ed's body, in plain view. The wallet contained a copy of the most incriminating letter Arthur had ever written. If Mrs. Hull had committed the murder, it might not occur to her to look inside Ed's wallet. Or, perhaps she did think of it and planted the letter there.

The fact Ed felt he needed his revolver for protection in the den is significant. He was afraid someone could hurt him, even inside his own house. He said he did not fear Arthur, so perhaps he was afraid someone else would break into the house and harm him or his family. On the other hand, he may have been afraid of someone in the house.

The murderer would have been covered in blood after the murder, but apart from a single smeared fingerprint near the door, there were no signs of droplets on the floor or the walls outside the immediate area where Ed was killed. Police knew the killer moved around the house to stage the scene after the murder, and had made at least two trips to get items from the pantry and open the kitchen window. How could that be done without leaving bloody footprints and blood droplets on the floor?

The only plausible explanation is that the killer changed their clothing after killing Ed. Once in clean clothes, they could move about freely without worrying about leaving a trail of blood. Yet there was no trace of bloody clothing in the Burdick house or in the Pennell home.

The answer may have been provided by Alfred Brookman, the elderly man who worked on the Burdick's furnace. He told detectives that the fire was surprisingly low. He knew the furnace was functioning correctly because he had worked on it earlier in the week. Maggie Murray heard Ed shoveling coal into the furnace around 10:30 p.m. The fire would still be burning at 10 a.m. the following morning, but the furnace was barely running when Alfred arrived. He was especially puzzled because Katie told him she had shoveled some coal into the furnace that morning.

It makes sense that the murderer took Ed's papers to the cellar to destroy them in the furnace. Afterwards, they tossed their bloody clothing in too, knowing the garments would burn to ashes by morning, even if they smothered the flames to a large degree.

After killing Ed, staging the scene, and looking through the victim's papers, the last act of the murderer was to turn off the gaslight in the room and close the den door. When Dr. Marcy entered the room hours later, he stumbled to the window because the room was in total darkness. Ensuring all of the lights were off before leaving the room would be odd behavior for an intruder. It is something that a person living in the home might do without thinking.

The youngest daughter of Ed and Alice Burdick was 10 years old when her father was murdered. In the morning, before Ed's body was discovered, she said she heard someone go downstairs just before the servants were up. She thought it was her father. If she was right, the person she heard walking downstairs must have either opened the door and window, or observed they were standing open and did not close them, despite the freezing February temperatures.

If Mrs. Hull murdered Ed, why would she wait until the household was awakening before opening the door and window? According to her account, Mrs. Hull locked her bedroom door at night before going to sleep. If she was the killer, it is difficult to imagine she would have opened the door and window at 2:00 a.m., just after Ed died, and allowed them to remain open and unguarded until just after 7:00 a.m. More likely, she would have returned to her bedroom and waited until she heard Maggie or Katie stir upstairs. Then she would have stolen downstairs and opened the door and window, knowing they would be discovered and closed in a matter of minutes.

Justice Murphy's declaration that Ed Burdick's character was sterling was no doubt correct and well-deserved. Much of what we know about Ed tells us he was a good man, known for his generosity and kindness. But he did have flaws, and they cost him dearly. For instance, in everything related to his divorce from Alice, he was weak and vacillating. He threatened to divorce his wife in May 1901, January 1902, December 1902, and possibly other times. Ed's reluctance to act was almost certainly a major contributing factor in his murder.

Alice inflicted a deep wound upon her family, but instead of treating it properly, Ed allowed the situation to drag on for years while the wound became infected, spreading into the bloodstream of everyone connected with the case, until the situation grew intolerable. The divorce certainly wasn't Ed's fault, but had he been confident and resolute and gotten his divorce the first—or even the second—time he threatened to, the murder might never have happened.

Whether the murderer was Mrs. Hull or Arthur Pennell, the motive for the crime revolved around Alice Burdick. Who was this woman who had wrought so much misery without ever getting her hands dirty?

Arthur told Alice that his love for her was greater than hers for him, which was true. After Ed was dead and Alice reinstalled herself at the house on Ashland Avenue, she seemed to lose all interest in Arthur. When she learned of his horrific death, she replied coldly, "Is that so? We hadn't heard."

Alice was photographed the night before she testified at the inquest into Ed's death

At the inquest, Alice listened, without emotion, as Arthur's promises to her of his eternal love and devotion were read aloud. When the DA and the judge openly speculated he had murdered Ed, destroying the reputation he had held so dear, Alice did not defend him. In fact, she took care to deflect any criticism of her conduct onto him. Everything was Arthur's fault: Arthur, who was willing to die for an hour in her company.

Alice's affair with Pennell had wrecked her home, devastated her husband, shamed her mother, and injured her children. Each time she was confronted, she disclaimed all responsibility and blamed everything on Arthur or Ed. When her husband forced her to leave in 1901, her letters to him seemed to taunt him, even as she pleaded to be allowed to come home. She promised, each time she was caught, never to let it happen again—yet she never had any intention of ending the affair.

When Ed accused her of wanting to come home only until Arthur would marry her, Alice vehemently denied it. But he was right. She used everyone around her, especially her husband, whose happiness she utterly destroyed.

Alice was truthful when she said she had no love for her husband. In early April, the *Baltimore Sun* reporter described her carefree demeanor as she showed him around the house. He noted that the sorrowful expression she had worn at the inquest had been discarded.

In 1903, the police had no forensic teams to search for microscopic evidence the killer left behind. Alice was free to have the den cleaned and put back in order as soon as the police left the house on Friday, February 27. The Burdicks had full-time servants who could have thoroughly cleaned the den in a day or two.

Instead, more than five weeks later, the den appeared just as it had on the morning of February 27, when her husband's battered body was found there. The presence of the ruined divan, covered in dried blood and brain matter, did not trouble Alice. She encouraged the reporter to take a look in the den, as though the macabre scene was an amusing curiosity. It's inexplicable that Alice would leave the den in such a state, particularly when her young children could have peaked into the room and suffered permanent trauma as a result.

Justice Murphy said of Alice, "Great as her wrong has been, great is her punishment." Her punishment, legally speaking, was the negative public attention the inquest caused and the official condemnation expressed by the court. The judge's censure did not appear to faze her in the least.

It's possible that Alice and her mother conspired to murder Ed. It's also possible that Mrs. Hull took matters into her own hands, without consulting her daughter, and then kept quiet about it. If she did murder Ed, Mrs. Hull may not have trusted her daughter with the information. Alice seemed pleased that Ed was out of the way, but if she were questioned by police, Mrs. Hull may have worried her daughter would betray her. Alice, after all, consistently sacrificed those who loved her to avoid anything resembling discomfort for herself.

Her cold heart never faltered.

The End

Note from the Author

Word-of-mouth is crucial for any author to succeed. If you enjoyed *Cold Heart*, please leave a review online—anywhere you are able. Even if it's just a sentence or two. It would make all the difference and would be very much appreciated.

Thanks!
Kimberly

About the Author

Kimberly Tilley is a Bay Area author who writes true stories of forgotten crimes from the early twentieth century. Her first book, *The Poisoned Glass* (2019), was an Amazon category #1 best-seller in four countries and multiple categories, including True Crime and American History. *Cold Heart* (2020) is her second book.

Kimberly is the co-founder of Pivot Discovery Career Services. She loves her work as a coach, and helping people create their ideal career.

You can read more of Kimberly's work at OldSpirituals.com.

Citations

I. "Killed by an Auto," The Morning News (Wilmington, DE), Aug. 27, 1902.

II. "Historical Statistics of the United States, Colonial Times to 1970, Bicentennial Edition, Part 2," US. Bureau of the Census, Washington, D.C., 1975 https://www.census.gov/history/pdf/histstats-colonial-1970.pdf.

III. "1902 Automobiles," Morris County (NJ) Library, https://mclib.info/reference/local-history-genealogy/historic-prices/1902-2/.

IV. "Rev. Levi M. Powers, in defense of Mrs. Hull, tacitly charges murder to man now dead," The Buffalo Review (Buffalo, NY), Mar. 16, 1903.

V. "Mrs. Burdick," The Semi-Weekly Messenger (Wilmington, NC), Mar. 27, 1903.

VI. "Burdick Murder Inquest has Fixed Guilt on None," The Philadelphia Inquirer (Philadelphia, PA) March 27, 1903. 1.

VII. "Burdick Inquest," Buffalo Evening News (Buffalo, NY), Mar. 25, 1903.

VIII. "Adultery and Divorce," Divorce Source. https://www.divorcesource.com/ds/divorceprocess/adultery-and-divorce-307.shtml. Accessed Jan 21, 2020.

IX. Detroit Publishing Co, C. C. & Detroit Publishing Co, P. (ca. 1900) The Waldorf-Astoria, New York. New York New York State New York. United States, ca. 1900. [Photograph] Retrieved from the Library of Congress Jan. 20, 2020., https://www.loc.gov/item/2016801904/.

X. "Pennell Shadowed Burdick," The Sun (NY, NY), Mar. 20, 1903.

XI. "Guilt Still Hidden," The Baltimore Sun (Baltimore, MD), Mar. 17, 1903.

XII. Arthur Forrest. Buffalo's Tragic Mystery the Famous Burdick Case and Its Thrilling Details. The Greatest Murder Sensation. 1903.

XIII. "Clues to Murderer!", Buffalo Morning Express and Illustrated Buffalo Express (Buffalo, NY), Feb. 28, 1903.

XIV. "Mysterious Burdick Murder Clues Lead to Nothing Tangible," The Buffalo Enquirer (Buffalo, NY), Feb. 28, 1903.

XXXV. Paul MacMahon. "The Inquest and the Virtues of Soft Adjudication" Aug. 25, 2014. http://online.wsj.com/public/resources/documents/inquest.pdf

XXXVI. "Mrs. Paine is Very Indignant," The Buffalo Enquirer (Buffalo, NY), Mar. 6, 1903.

XXXVII. "Loved Him Dearly But Showed Little Concern," The Buffalo Courier (Buffalo, NY), Mar. 17, 1903.

XXXVIII. "Rev. L.M. Powers Lays the Blame at Pennell's Door," The Buffalo Times (Buffalo, NY), Mar. 16, 1903.

XXXIX. "Dr. Marcy Explains Talk of Suicide," The Buffalo Times (Buffalo, NY), Mar. 16, 1903.

XL. "Mrs. Paine Tells of Her Meetings with Burdick," The Evening World (NY, NY), Mar. 17, 1903.

XLI. Blames Pennell. The Baltimore Sun (Baltimore, MD). Mar 18, 1903.

XLII. "I Know Why Papa was Sick," The Buffalo Review (Buffalo, NY), Mar. 25, 1903.

XLIII. "Mrs. Burdick Admits Much," Times Union (Brooklyn, NY), Mar. 24, 1903.

XLIV. "Done with Mrs. Burdick," Buffalo Morning Express and Illustrated Buffalo Express (Buffalo, NY), Mar. 25, 1903.

XLV. "Who Killed Edwin Burdick?" The Buffalo Enquirer (Buffalo, NY), Mar. 25, 1903.

XLVI. "Burdick Inquest Will Be Reopened to Hear Bartender," The Buffalo Courier (Buffalo, NY), Mar. 28, 1903.

XLVII. "Burdick Knew of Police Scandal," Francisco Examiner (San Francisco, CA), Mar. 30, 1903.

XLVIII. "No Show for Pennell," The Buffalo Commercial (Buffalo, NY), Apr. 1, 1903.

XLIX. "Who Went to the Den?" The Baltimore Sun, Apr. 6, 1903

L. "Still Resides in Buffalo," The Crowley Post-Signal (Crowley, LA), Jul. 29, 1903.

LI. "No Mystery in the Death of Dr. Paine." The Buffalo Enquirer, Dec.12, 1904

Thank you so much for reading one of **Kimberly Tilley's** novels.
If you enjoyed the experience, please check out our recommended
title for your next great read!

The Poisoned Glass by Kimberly Tilley

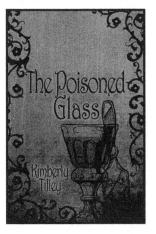

"A great read and a fascinating retelling of a long-forgotten
murder, that still resonates to this very day...
for anybody interested in the history of the Silk City!"
–Mark S. Auerbach, City Historian, Passaic, New Jersey

BLACK✸ROSE
writing™

Made in the USA
Las Vegas, NV
04 January 2023

64899035R00134